SACRAMENTO PUBLIC LIBRARY

3 3029 06575 1059

D0396660

SACRAMENTO PUBLIC LIBRARY
828 "I" STREET
SACRAMENTO, CA 95814
6/2011

Renegade for Peace and Justice

Renegade for Peace and Justice

Congresswoman Barbara Lee Speaks for Me

Barbara Lee

ROWMAN & LITTLEFIELD PUBLISHERS, INC.
Lanham • Boulder • New York • Toronto • Plymouth, UK

ROWMAN & LITTLEFIELD PUBLISHERS, INC.

Published in the United States of America
by Rowman & Littlefield Publishers, Inc.
A wholly owned subsidiary of The Rowman & Littlefield Publishing Group, Inc.
4501 Forbes Boulevard, Suite 200, Lanham, Maryland 20706
www.rowmanlittlefield.com

Estover Road
Plymouth PL6 7PY
United Kingdom

Distributed by National Book Network

Copyright © 2008 by Barbara Lee

All rights reserved. No part of this publication may be reproduced,
stored in a retrieval system, or transmitted in any form or by any
means, electronic, mechanical, photocopying, recording, or otherwise,
without the prior permission of the publisher.

British Library Cataloguing in Publication Information Available

Library of Congress Cataloging-in-Publication Data

Lee, Barbara, 1946–
  Renegade for peace and justice : Congresswoman Barbara Lee speaks for me / Barbara
Lee.
     p. cm.
  Includes index.
  ISBN-13: 978-0-7425-5843-4 (cloth : alk. paper)
  ISBN-10: 0-7425-5843-6 (cloth : alk. paper)
  ISBN-13: 978-0-7425-6610-1 (pbk. : alk. paper)
  ISBN-10: 0-7425-6610-2 (pbk. : alk paper)
  eISBN-13: 978-0-7425-6565-4
  eISBN-10: 0-7425-6565-3
  1. Lee, Barbara, 1946– 2. Legislators—United States—Biography. 3. Legislators—
California—Biography. 4. African American legislators—Biography. 5. African
American legislators—California—Biography. 6. Women legislators—United States—
Biography. 7. Women legislators—California—Biography. 8. African American
women—Biography. 9. African American women—California—Biography. I. Title.
  E840.8.L37A3 2008
  328.73092—dc22
  [B]   2008015465

Printed in the United States of America

♾™ The paper used in this publication meets the minimum requirements of
American National Standard for Information Sciences—Permanence of Paper
for Printed Library Materials, ANSI/NISO Z39.48-1992.

To my beautiful, brilliant mother, *Mildred Massey*, who gave me my life.

To my sisters, *Mildred Whitfield* and *Beverly Hardy*—haven't we and aren't we having a ball? Both of you fill me with laughter and joy.

To my sons, *Tony* and *Craig Lee*—you make me so proud.

To my grandchildren, *Jordan, Joshua, Jonah*, and *Simone Lee*— you are amazing. Study hard.

To my friends—you are truly my friends.

To the "butterflies". . . you know who you are . . . stay bold and beautiful.

To my staff, present and past—my dreams and efforts are not only mine but ours. I could not do it without you.

To "Team Lee"—you are changing the world.

To my aunties, *Juanita Franklin* and *Lois Murrell*—thank you for your love.

To *Peggy Lee*, whose generosity will always be remembered.

To all of my daddies, my grandmothers and grandfathers, especially *Papa*, thank you for loving me.

To all of my ancestors—you paved the way.

To Ron Dellums—thank you for believing in me.

To my entire family, my constituents, and my colleagues—your support is deeply appreciated.

To Bono, Mike Honda, Dolores Huerta, Pastor Smith, Gloria Steinem, Alice Walker—all of you are incredible spirits. Thank you for your kindness.

And to the awesome God that I worship—thy will be done.

Contents

Acknowledgments	ix
Introduction	xi
Chapter 1	1
Chapter 2	25
Chapter 3	45
Chapter 4	65
Chapter 5	77
Chapter 6	101
Chapter 7	125
Chapter 8	147
Chapter 9	167
Chapter 10	187

Conclusion   201

Index   209

About the Author   223

Acknowledgments

Thank you, Helen Thomas and Elihu Harris, for inspiring me to take this on. To Rowman & Littlefield, especially Chris, your belief in me is deeply appreciated. To my editor, Mary Beth Hebert, thank you for meeting the challenge. To Summer Whitford, I could not have done this without you. To my friends, Carol Williams, Bobby Seale, Alice Walker, and Gale Kaufman, and my pastor, the Rev. Dr. J. Alfred Smith Sr., your insights were remarkable. And to my agent, Diane Nine, your patience, understanding, and professionalism are deeply appreciated.

Introduction

> Never think you are alone when you stand for right because
> GOD is with you. We are very proud of you. It makes us feel
> good that you are a Congressional Member.

Rosa Parks wrote these kind words to me in a letter some years ago,
and when I read these two sentences I was so moved that a woman
of her stature—and a hero in her own right—felt that I was carrying the torch for peace and the nonviolent struggle for human
rights. By sharing my life story with others, I want to help people
realize that bad choices, adversity, and all of the other obstacles life
places before us can be overcome. There is always hope! Rosa Parks
was the mother of the civil rights movement, and her willingness
to put her life on the line in the face of threats and violence confirmed for me that each time I stood up for what was right, I was
never truly alone. No, standing behind me was God and the teachings of Christ. Moreover, I was standing on the shoulders of gi-
ants—all the people who came before me who risked it all and
whose bravery and sheer force of will changed the face of history.
These freedom fighters' quests to end war, fight poverty, eradicate

injustice, and eliminate discrimination continue to be shining beacons for us all, and their causes have not dimmed with the passage of time. I have drawn strength from their courage and indomitable spirits. Rosa Parks' single act of defiance created a storm of bigoted fury and retaliation, yet she always remained a pillar of calm and determination. Her peaceful resistance inspired her contemporaries and led to a true civil rights movement that continues to galvanize new generations—and she has been a reminder to me that one person truly can make a difference.

I never set out to be a champion for peace or human rights or to chart new territory by going against the tide. But like Esther of the Old Testament, I was taught that if I witnessed an injustice, then I had no choice but to stand and be counted. I had to do something. To do nothing has never been an option for me, and if it fell to me to lead, then that was the path destined for me. I have been fortunate to have met, worked with, or read about incredible people who have shown me that having faith and doing what is right is its own reward. I certainly never consciously decided to become a lightning rod of political controversy. Each time I have been thrust into the center of conflict, it has been the hands of fate at work and my sincere wish to follow my conscience and to right a wrong. I often wonder what my life would have been like if I hadn't met or worked with some of my most important influences and mentors, like the Catholic Sisters of Loretto, Reps. Shirley Chisholm (D-NY) and Ron Dellums (D-CA)—now mayor of Oakland, California, Gloria Steinem, Bobby Seale, and Dolores Huerta. No one accomplishes anything completely alone in life, and I have been blessed by a wonderful loving family and friends who have supported me. My faith also has helped me face each new challenge. I have been fortunate to receive recognition for my work throughout my life, and these confirmations of personal and professional accomplishments have sustained me as well. It started in high school when I won a

Bank of America Achievement Award and a Rotary Club Music scholarship. Later, going to Mills College became a positive and enriching, life-altering experience that instilled me with the confidence I needed to achieve my goals.

When I worked on Rep. Chisholm's (D-NY) campaign for President, I saw firsthand that there were important women of color who could give young black women an idea of just how far they could go in life if they worked hard and never lost faith in themselves. Had I not so admired "Mrs. C," as she was affectionately known, I might not have worked on her campaign and not have had the chance to meet my future mentor and boss, Rep. Dellums (D-CA). His faith in my abilities gave me the work experience of a lifetime and enabled me to become one of the first African American women as a top key staffer. During my eleven years in his office, I watched him take unpopular stances on peace, the war in Vietnam, and the issues of race, poverty, and human rights. I saw how he struggled with his conscience and how he often stood alone for or against an important issue. When he resigned from the House of Representatives in 1998, I was able to run for his seat and carry the baton, which he passed to me, for the work he had begun. Winning his seat has been a professional and personal milestone in many ways. I became the first woman to be elected to represent the Ninth District of California, which includes Albany, Ashland, Berkeley, Castro Valley, Cherryland, Emeryville, Fairview, Oakland, and Piedmont.

As a member of the House of Representatives I have worked hard to represent my district and the American people. Like Ron, I have been forced to make difficult votes that have earned me the admiration of many and the hatred of some. In some cases my votes famously foisted me on to the front pages and into the history books, but I try to vote for what is right. Being in the limelight can be a blessing if you are trying to bring attention to an issue, but it can also be dangerous and frightening. My vote against giving the Bush administration a "blank check" to use force after 9/11 didn't feel momentous—just morally, ethically, and constitutionally correct. It never occurred to me that I would be the only person voting against it. I had made other controversial votes like that when the Clinton administration wanted to use force in Kosovo. Again I was the sole "no" vote, and I am sure that in the future I will vote for or against a bill that will earn me the enmity of other members of Congress and the public. But each time I contemplate taking on a difficult cause that is sure to be met with resistance and strife, I know that I can persevere if I remember who else faced dogged opposition, whether it was my mother who fought her own battles to do the right thing or Rosa Parks.

Mahatma Gandhi was a man whose method of nonviolent resistance and civil disobedience introduced the Western World to a new way of bringing about change and created in India a free and democratic nation of 300 million people, where once there had been colonial oppression and subjugation. I was very moved when I visited his burial site and house in Mumbai, India, several years ago.

Martin Luther King, Jr. saw the dignity and power of Gandhi and Rosa Parks' actions and began a groundswell of political action that would change American history.

Gloria Steinem changed the dialogue about women and the future of the women's movement by challenging what it meant to be a woman and a feminist. She showed us that as women, it's up to us to define ourselves, not men, or society, government, advertisers, or the media.

Dolores Huerta, the mother of the United Farm Workers Union, has for 40 years used nonviolent resistance to fight for the rights of farm workers, women, legal immigrants, and Latinos, and she did it in a time when Latinos were still considered indentured servants by many Americans. She has been arrested more than 20 times and has been brutally beaten by police only to return and resume her struggles with grace and dignity. I have worked with her, marched with her, and greatly admire her struggles and accomplishments.

Bono, the lead singer for the rock band U2, could have sat back and enjoyed the money, fame, and opportunity that his success afforded him. Instead, he has decided to work with politicians like myself, former Sen. Jesse Helms (R-NC), Speaker of the House Nancy Pelosi (D-CA) and President George W. Bush to try to end the senseless and unnecessary spread of the HIV/AIDS pandemic and to help treat and cure the millions of people dying in Africa. Every time I talk with him, I feel his heart and his soul.

Each of these people, in his or her own way, has left a mark on the world. I hope that by telling my story, other people are encouraged to follow in our footsteps and help make the world a more compassionate, safer, cleaner, and healthier place to live. Throughout my political career, I have brought my training as a social worker to my work confronting the challenges that face the people of my district, across the nation, and throughout the world. I have tried to build bipartisan coalitions to protect the fundamental human rights of all people: health care, housing, education, jobs, and the quest to create livable communities in a peaceful world. I am merely carrying on the work begun by others, and I hope to pass the baton to the next generation who can continue my work to represent the voice of reason in the campaign to reshape our national budget and our vision for what America will look like in the future. If we choose, Americans can reclaim our lost esteem and prove to the world that we are a nation of people who value freedom and condemn any attempt to shackle or stifle expression. I try to live by a code that respects life and recognizes that our diversity is a strength that should be celebrated, not a weakness that should divide us. When we are divided by fear, hatred, ignorance, and lack of understanding, we cannot live in harmony with other nations. My philosophy on life, politics, government, and the fight for peace and justice has been guided by tenets wonderfully expressed by one of the great leaders of our century, the Dalai Lama, who once said

> Peace, in the sense of the absence of war, is of little value to someone who is dying of hunger or cold. It will not remove the pain of torture inflicted on a prisoner of conscience. It does not comfort those who have lost their loved ones in floods caused by senseless deforestation in a neighbouring country. Peace can only last where human rights are respected, where the people are fed, and where individuals and nations are free.[1]

Notes

1. Dalai Lama, "Nobel Lecture," Nobelprize.org, December 11, 1989. For the full text see <http://nobelprize.org/nobel_prizes/peace/laureates/1989/lama-lecture.html>.

Chapter One

I always wanted to be somebody. If I made it, it's half because I was game enough to take a lot of punishment along the way and half because there were a lot of people who cared enough to help me.

—Althea Gibson

Summertime in El Paso, Texas, can seem like a never-ending sentence of punishing heat, and July 16, 1946, was no exception. As sweltering and miserable as it was that day though, it still didn't compare to the white searing waves of labor pains that were ripping through Mildred's swollen body as she entered Hotel Dieu with her mother Willie. Named for the famous seventeenth century hospital for the poor in Paris, this local hospital had been founded by the Daughters of Charity of St. Vincent de Paul, gentle nuns who for more than three centuries had taken care of the forgotten people of society—slaves, the aged, the poor, the mentally ill, and the infirm. Unfortunately, in 1946 air-conditioning was a cool blessing that was still years away in the future, and the weather made the hospital's rooms and hallways feel suffocating and confining.

Around this time of year, people usually tried to stay in the shade as much as possible and laid low until the reprieve of sunset. As unforgiving as the heat was, it wasn't nature's cruelty that was making Mildred's labor so difficult to withstand that day, or putting her life and the life of her unborn child at risk. It was the racist and inhumane treatment Mildred was subjected to in Hotel Dieu. The dehumanizing lack of compassion and empathy shown by the nurses and doctors was appalling; it was as if their solemn oath as caregivers, part of which says they must "keep the sick free from harm and injustice," was reserved for only white people.

Willie spent hours trying to convince the admissions office that her darker-skinned daughter came from Irish roots, so that way she could be admitted into the hospital to deliver her baby by Cesarean section. Even though Willie also gave the name of the white doctor, Dr. Stafford, who delivered Mildred at Providence Hospital, Mildred wasn't white enough to be admitted to the "whites-only" hospital. It wasn't that long before 1946 that this country had written policies that dictated that even if you had just "one drop" of black blood in you, you were black. As each agonizing minute ticked by, Mildred could do nothing but writhe in pain and patiently wait to see if she could finally be seen by a doctor. After raising hell, Willie finally succeeded in getting the hospital to call Mildred's OB-GYN, and he told the hospital staff to admit her, which they did. But they didn't do much more than that; they left Mildred lying in the hall on a bed and ignored her as they went about their business.

You see, Mildred was a fair-skinned "colored" woman, but Willie could pass for white, and it was Willie's confounding "whiteness" that was giving the racist admitting nurses and doctors such problems. Throughout American history, some fair-skinned black people, or as they were called during the 1940s and 1950s, "colored" people, passed themselves off as white and lived undetected in white society. Right or wrong, "passing" was often the only way slaves could find freedom or blacks could get access to the same educational and job opportunities available to whites. These black people paid a high price for living a dangerous life of lies and secrets. It's hard to imagine what it must have been like for them—they lived and benefited from their white status yet were forced to stand by in silence as their friends and relatives struggled to just survive in a society where black people were treated as second class at best and at the worst were considered merely chattel, to be bought and sold at will. For more than four hundred years the lives of black people in America had been separate, but they were never equal.

As the wait for treatment perilously dragged on, Mildred's condition became more unstable, and the life of her unborn child hung in the balance. Mildred's labor was complicated by the fact that she needed a Cesarean. By the time the callous people at the hospital finally agreed to help Mildred with the birth, the doctors were forced into a last-minute forceps delivery. It turns out that Mildred's baby was a little girl, and as they grasped her head to try to ease it along the birth canal, the forceps dug into the soft tender flesh of her head which caused a tear above her right eye, or I should say my eye, because that little baby girl was me. Most of the scar is long since gone, but when I think about how and why it got there and about the disgraceful way my mother was treated, it just reaffirms my resolve to make things better for women and people of color. I am determined to make it so no one, whether they are women, people of color, or with any other kind of ethnic or religious distinction, should ever have to go through the horrible ordeal that my mother endured.

Although I consider myself a proud African American woman, that scar has been a constant reminder of where I came from and that no matter how much black people have accomplished, it was still less than forty years ago when we couldn't even share a bathroom, drinking fountain, or classroom with whites. Less than a century ago, black people were treated with little more regard than farm animals. This history keeps me grounded and is part of why I work so hard for my constituents and our great country. It is why I try to fight injustice wherever I see it, no matter how uncomfortable it may be for me. I am especially sensitive to the plight of the poor and the underrepresented people in my district, the Ninth California District, a place that I have been proud to serve as a Congresswoman since 1998. I believe I have a responsibility to fight for many of these same issues on a global front. My name is Barbara Lee, and this is just the beginning of my story.

Like so many African Americans, the legacy of slavery and sexual abuse that has been heaped upon generations of women in my family tree is evident in our physical features. My heritage is a complex mix of black, white, and Native American relatives. Unlike many people who like to think of grandparents and great-grandparents as loving figures who dote on their grandchildren, it has always been painful and embarrassing for me to acknowledge the degrading stain of rape and exploitation that can be traced back to some of my white ancestors, especially on my mother's side. It's heart wrenching to think of the fear and pain exacted on the women of my family by violent, predatory bigots. For centuries their power over my people was not only above question, it was an accepted way of life. My great-grandmother, Grandma Charlotte, lived in a time when black women were at the mercy of their white male owners. She was part of the household of a white Irishman in New Orleans, Louisiana. He raped her repeatedly. She was powerless to say or do anything about it. Over the years, she bore him several children, one of whom was my beautiful grandmother Willie Pointer.

Neither regarded as white or black, both my grandmother Willie and my mother Mildred had fair skin and could easily "pass." Our family's Irish bloodline is visible in my handsome grandsons Joshua and Jonah, too. When they were just little boys they had flaming red hair and even now their hair has beautiful red tones. Despite all of the terrible things that my family has had to bear, I had a happy childhood surrounded by loving relatives who made sure I wanted for nothing and that I received a wonderful education. My family brought me up to appreciate the value of work, and our devotion to the Church and abiding faith in God spurred me on to try to do His work. It's from my faith that I derive my strength because I know that every challenge that God has given me has been a test, and no matter what the obstacle, He has never given me more than He thought I could handle.

The El Paso of my childhood was a thriving town and had been so for quite a while because in the nineteenth century the Mexican Revolution had led to an exodus of refugees fleeing the turmoil across the border. During the first quarter of the twentieth century, the city continued to grow, except for a slow period during the Depression in the 1930s. Things picked right back up again following World War II, and development at Fort Bliss in the 1940s and 1950s was one of the reasons many people, including my family, lived in the area. This raised the number of residents to 130,003 in 1950, and by 1960, El Paso's population had more than doubled, totaling 276,687. Despite these numbers, it was still less than 3 percent black when I was growing up.

My beloved, late father, Garvin Tutt was one of those people who came to El Paso following the war. A short man with sort of reddish-brown dark skin, he looked handsome and dignified in his Army uniform. He had attended St. Emma's, an all boys' Catholic military high school in Rock Castle, Virginia, and after graduating, he joined the Army as a private. By the time he met my mother he had been promoted to sergeant and was soon sent to OCS, Officer Candidate School, at Fort Riley, Kansas. After OCS, he became a second lieutenant and returned to my mother a changed man. From that day forward my mother said he became arrogant, overly formal, outwardly secure, and sort of uppity. But I don't see him as uppity; to me he was just a typical proud black man who loved his job as a computer operations manager in the Army and took pleasure showing off his three girls. Like most Army men, my dad was stationed in a variety of places, sometimes with his family and sometimes without us. Whenever he could, he brought us with him, and he made sure that we rarely lived on the Army post. Instead we lived in a real house. The few times we did live on base, it was for less than a year—like the time we lived on Fort Bliss because my father wanted to save some money. Or when we lived on Fort Lewis for six months when my dad was stationed in Washington State. Or the time we lived in Berkeley, California, when my father was stationed at Fort Ord in Monterey.

Unfortunately, while we lived in El Paso, my father and mother's marriage suffered, and their problems seemed to just get worse with time. My father was strict not just with us girls, but with my mother too, and he had a ton of rules for us all. For starters, he never wanted us to associate with noncommissioned officers (NCOs) or their kids, even though it was okay for him to spend every payday shooting dice with the enlisted men in their barracks. He wanted to control what his three girls did and imposed restrictions on my mother, like not letting her wear high heels and forcing her to wear glasses. There were many scenes where my mother and father would have loud arguments, my father would lash out, and then my mother would fight back by throwing or breaking things. I remember once when my father's sister Aunt Evelyn came to visit us. We were having dinner, and everything was calm and normal at the table. I was using my bread to sop up the gravy on my plate, which for some reason made my father so angry that out of the blue he rolled up a newspaper and hit me with it like I was a puppy. This, of course, made my mother angry, and in retaliation she threw a glass bottle of water at him. She then grabbed me and my sisters, ran out of the house, and took us to stay with one of my aunts who lived nearby.

As much as the constant bickering was tearing their marriage apart, my mother was still willing to stick it out and try to make the marriage work. For a while my father was stationed in Japan, without us. While stationed there he met a Japanese woman named Reiko and began having an affair with her. Unlucky for him, however, it just so happened that two of my mother's friends as well as my godmother were stationed in Japan at the same time. My godmother ran into my father often and discovered that he was not only having an affair with this woman, but was openly dating her and that they were going out together, acting as a couple. My godmother let my mother know what was going on. Still my mother was ready to forgive him and take him back. On one of his furloughs to the States, he stopped in to see us in El Paso, and then left to pay a visit to his mother, Grandmother Echols, who lived in Missouri. As chance would have it, the day after he left, a letter from Japan arrived for him at the house, and it was the contents of this letter that would be the last straw for my mother.

Curious to see what the letter contained, and probably suspecting that it was from his Japanese girlfriend, my mother had our housekeeper Lupe steam it open so she could read it. Sure enough, it was from Reiko and included intimate details of their time together and a picture of her in a white dress that he had bought for her. My father was an amateur camera buff and loved to take pictures and movies. My dad returned to Japan, and about a year later, upon his return to the United States, not knowing we had read the letter, he was showing slides of Japan at my Aunt Juanita and Uncle Albert's house. These slides were of Japan and some of the people he had met, and low and behold, here was a picture of a lady in a white dress. My sister immediately screamed, "That's the white dress!" No one said anything, but right then and there, mother decided their marriage was really over. Her lawyer, Mr. Knollenberg, filed for divorce and said that the letter and picture was all that she needed. She mailed the divorce papers with the letter to my father who had left El Paso and gone to Missouri to visit his mother. Less than six months later, my parents' divorce was finalized.

My dad married Reiko in 1957, and while they lived in El Paso I occasionally stayed with them on weekends. When they moved out to Long Beach, California, I would stay with them during the summer. I watched closely how my father treated Reiko. He was very chauvinistic and insisted she do all the housework and be the best hostess at their bridge and dinner parties, which she was. She was a great cook and excellent housekeeper and sewed skirts for school for my sisters and me. My dad was a big dog lover, and I remember his boxer named Duchess and later on he had a large poodle named Princess—I loved my father and Reiko very much. The same year my dad married Reiko, my mother married another Army officer, Bill Massey. I was eleven at the time, and Bill Massey was a handsome man who showered my mother with gifts and became a good stepfather to my sisters and me. He had a good heart and did things like drive us out to California for summer vacations with Auntie Nita and Uncle Albert. And he was generous with presents at birthdays and Christmas—what little girl wouldn't have been thrilled to receive fancy Madame Alexander dolls? We affectionately called Bill "Bugs," a nickname he earned when he sent us a photo of himself from his tour of duty in Germany. In the photo Bill was wearing a big coat with a hood on that made him look like a rabbit. Bill, unfortunately, was a womanizer, and he and Mother constantly argued about his inability to manage money. Too, he was terrible with money and made a mess of my mother's finances. He often lied about expenses and bounced checks but despite the problems with money, I believe my mother really loved him. After all she was with him off and on, for 18 years.

Both of my mother's marriages to Army men often left her living alone with us girls because during each of her marriages my father and stepfather were frequently stationed elsewhere. My mother's father, William, "W. C." Calhoun Parish, or as we called him, Papa, was my father figure when I was growing up. In El Paso my mother, my two sisters Mildred and Beverly, and I lived with my Papa and my grandmother Willie Parish. Papa and Willie's house on Yandell Boulevard was a nice three-bedroom ranch that had a screened in back porch with a good-sized back yard surrounded by a chain-link fence. Our garage was in the back alley, and in the front, our house had a nice big porch that looked out onto a pretty yard full of flowers, red rose bushes, and two palm trees.

Papa was an extraordinary man, and he had a big impact on me. He was striking to look at too, because his features were clearly Native American and African American. He also spoke Spanish fluently, was very smart, and had a degree in liberal arts from Houston-Tillotson College in Austin, Texas. Papa was not afraid of a challenge and he became the first African American letter carrier in El Paso, a job he proudly held for 35 years. He was interested in all sorts of things, from gardening to improving the lot of black people. Our house was always buzzing with activity. There was a constant stream of his friends from church or the lodge, coming and going through our front door. Papa was active in the NAACP, enjoyed taking care of church business, and loved being involved in the Masons. He not only regularly attended meetings at Prince Hall Masonic Lodge Number 53 where he was a member, but he was the treasurer and a 33rd degree Mason, an honorary degree that is conferred for exceptional service. It was his love of gardening that made our front yard so bright and colorful. He took pleasure from simple things in life, like the Eagle brand of condensed milk that he drank in his coffee every morning, his insistence on buying butcher-cut meat, the satisfaction he got from growing his own vegetables, and his walks to the Five Points area of town several times a week to buy his favorite peach ice cream at Price's Ice Cream Parlor.

Papa was strict with his girls, and that included my mom, not just me and my sisters. He didn't approve of staying up late, cigarette smoking, or laziness. Although my mom was a grown woman with children, he made it clear that keeping late hours was not allowed and for years my mother hid her cigarette smoking from Papa. He may have been strict about some things, but he was a soft touch at heart and a loving, caring man. Papa was more bark than bite, and although he had a light tan, splintery wooden stick he threatened to use on us, he never did. I really don't remember many spankings at all.

I am the oldest child in my family; my sister Mildred was born almost 14 months after me. We have always been as thick as thieves, and when we were growing up we were inseparable. We have shared a lot together as friends and sisters. Even our first children were born around the same time: Mildred's son was born exactly a week before my son Tony. We did everything together as girls. We played with our collection of movie-star paper dolls. We played house, and we made Mulberry pies with mud and leaves picked from the Mulberry tree in the yard. We even ate a few of them! In Papa's garden Mildred and I planted watermelons and beans along the backyard fence that we shared with our neighbor, Mr. Washington and his daughter, Carlottia, who was my best friend. In addition to gardening, Mildred and I had a rich full childhood and participated in a Tom Thumb wedding at the Myrtle Avenue Church, performed in pageants and plays, went on hayrides, went square dancing, and had a great time at an endless number of cookouts.

Mildred and Beverly were typical kids—always teasing me and conning me into doing their housework because they knew I was a real pushover. I always stood up for them and covered up their bad behavior, but I could also have a bad temper that I worked hard to keep under wraps. I was only five when my youngest sister Beverly was born, and I don't remember much about that time except that when my mother came home from the hospital she was wearing a dark blue suit. When she came into the house she placed Beverly, who was in her bassinette, on a piano stool and all I could do was stand there mesmerized. I stared at my new baby sister for a long time and was amazed at how fair-skinned she was, just like my mother, even though she grew up to be a beautiful chocolate brown. I remember always feeling very self-conscious about my appearance and as a young black girl I lacked self-esteem. All of this emphasis on skin color and hair made me envious of my mother's coloring and appearance which is why I used to show off my attractive mother. It somehow made me feel better. My mother was naturally beautiful with long reddish brown hair, pale skin, and green eyes, just like my grandmother Willie.

When I was growing up, most people mistakenly thought that my mother was Mexican, which she got a kick out of. The problem was, my father didn't find it so amusing and when the two of them would walk down the street together, men would stare at her. My father didn't like the ogling, but that didn't stop my mother from teasing him, "It's not because they think I am Mexican, but because I am pretty." She took great care with her grooming, often crossing the border into Juarez, Mexico, to get her hair and nails done. I remember her manicures were only fifty cents, and no one had a mother prettier than mine. She is in her 80s now and is still a beautiful woman. The one trait that I got from my mother was her hair, which was fairly long. As a child, folks told me I was lucky to have "good hair," meaning it wasn't kinky and didn't have to be pressed. It was more like white people's hair. Yet I was also ashamed it wasn't as kinky as my black friends' hair. So much of my esteem and self-image was tied to other people's perceptions of beauty. It made me want to grow up fast so that I could become something or someone different. To look older, even before I had bras of my own, I would steal my mother's bras and stuff toilet paper in the cups.

I was never content with my looks or who I was as a person, and I always looked toward tomorrow, toward growing up. I learned to sew and make dresses that were more adult looking than my mother preferred. Everyone said I was sneaky, spoiled, and stubborn but that I also had a big heart and would do anything for anyone. I cried easily and was very sensitive, which often made my relatives say about me that "still waters run deep." I don't remember smiling a lot, and sometimes I think I was really depressed because I was too serious.

My mother had an eye for fashion and quality, and she loved to shop, often buying us expensive beautiful clothes with matching accessories. Once I had a red corduroy jumper that she wanted me to wear to school, but I didn't want to wear it. The only way I could think of getting out of wearing the outfit was to hide my matching red socks. When it was time to get dressed, my mother asked me where the red socks were. I was bound and determined not to have to wear the red jumper so I lied and told her I didn't know. She spanked me and even though I cried and cried, I refused to tell her where they were. That night, she woke me up around one o'clock in the morning and made me watch a television show about a little girl who lied to her parents and the bad things that happened to her as a result. The next day she made me wear the jumper—with white socks instead of red. When she reads this book she will finally find out what happened to the infamous red socks—I had thrown them behind the bathtub where no one could find them.

She always made sure we participated in extracurricular activities, and I can't remember wanting something I didn't get. In retrospect, she sacrificed a lot for us because she paid for our Catholic school tuition, piano, sewing, ballet lessons, and also Brownies and Girl Scouts. My Brownie troop was #101 and my Girl Scout troop was #151; I especially loved to sew, play the piano, and fence. Every summer she sent us to California to stay with Auntie Juanita and Uncle Albert. She played bridge, went to the Phillis Wheatley Club, Birthday Club meetings, church, Eastern Star Lodge meetings, and was a good cook. The Phillis Wheatley Club was especially important to my mother because it was a black women's social club and gave her access to a network of clubs around the country. From that association, she had a social network of friends and business contacts that gave her inspiring black female role models to look up to and emulate, not the least of which was the woman for whom the clubs were named, Phillis Wheatley.

Phillis Wheatley was a woman of inspiring talents and accomplishments. She became an African American woman of many important firsts in America: she was the first African American, the first slave, and the third woman in the United States to publish a book of poems. Phillis was born in Gambia in West Africa sometime between 1753 and 1755 and then kidnapped as a child and brought to America in shackles, where she was sold to John and Susanna Wheatley in Boston on July 11, 1761. Phillis was purchased by John Wheatley as a servant for his wife and very quickly her natural intelligence became apparent. Although between eight and ten years old at the time, Phillis quickly learned to speak English fluently and could read the Bible with ease. Susanna Wheatley developed a deep affection for young Phillis. Rather than have her become a domestic, Susanna encouraged her to study and acquire an education. Phillis studied theology as well as the Latin, Greek, and English classics and then in 1767, she published her first poem which was followed six years later by her book *Poems on Various Subjects*. As a reward for her talents, she was given her freedom by John Wheatley and as an adult became a woman of international renown. Phillis traveled abroad to promote her book. She was considered an important figure in her day and was a supporter of George Washington, so much so that she corresponded with him and wrote a poem in praise of him at the beginning of the Revolutionary War, a cause she strongly favored. As luck would have it, Phillis appeared before George Washington in March of 1776 and among her many admirers, was Voltaire, who referred to her "very good English verse." Although she supported the Revolutionary War, Phillis felt slavery to be the issue which separated whites from true heroism: "whites can not hope to find/Deivine acceptance with th' Almighty mind when they disgrace/And hold in bondage Afric's blameless race." This incredible and gifted woman is inspiring for her talents as a writer and poet and for her fortitude in an era when women were rarely treated as respected writers, and slaves most definitely did not read or become published authors. How remarkable and cruelly ironic it was that an African child named for *The Phillis*, the very same slave ship that brought her to America, would become a poet popular in the newly created country of the United States of America and abroad.

My mother's involvement in the Phillis Wheatley Club gave her the encouragement to stand on her own and helped her instill in us a respect for education, ambition, and a desire to succeed. She was pretty strict and wouldn't let me date until I was sixteen, and like other mothers at that time, she never taught my sisters and me about the birds and the bees, which would prove to be a problem for me when I reached adolescence. Education, music, and a strong work ethic were important to Papa. He worked hard his entire life, and he expected the same thing of his daughters and granddaughters. Papa had instilled in my mother a very strong work ethic and a determination to be successful. She attended a segregated but well-regarded public school in El Paso, and she graduated number three in her class of sixteen, the largest class ever at that time. After high school she received a scholarship to attend Houston-Tillotson College, a liberal arts college in Austin, Texas. She later transferred to Southern University in Baton Rouge, Louisiana, because Houston-Tillotson didn't have a business administration major. She also went to Prairie View College in Prairie View, Texas, for summer school. After segregation ended, she was one of the first black students to attend Texas Western College, which is now the University of Texas in El Paso.

I always remember my mother telling me about her time at Southern University when she pledged into the black sorority Alpha Kappa Alpha (AKA). Her roommate was a talented musician and wanted to join AKA but wasn't admitted because of her skin color—she was too dark. As part of the sorority pledging, every young woman was given a gold pin that was designed with the symbol of the sorority, which for the AKAs was an ivy. As pledges, the young women wore their pins on their clothes in fidelity with their sisters. My mother was appalled when she learned that a black sorority would discriminate against another black woman on the basis of the complexion of her skin. Her friend was refused admission to the sorority because the veins could not be seen on the inside of her wrist. In outrage, she threw away her ivy pledge pin and asked one of the sorority's more prominent members, a great woman who is revered in the struggle for civil and women's rights, Mary McLeod Bethune, to come to campus to deal with this travesty. Mrs. Bethune accepted my mother's invitation and came to campus to put things right. She informed the AKAs that if they did not change their policy about skin color, she would shut the chapter down. Needless to say, the policy was changed but my mother never rejoined because she said "they still had it in them."

When I was a child, my mother worked full time as a secretary for the USO from 3 p.m. to 11 p.m., which is why I spent so much time with my grandmother Willie and Papa and didn't get to spend as much time with her as I wanted. But we always had time with Papa, who insisted his girls have an appreciation and understanding of music. He made sure my sisters and I diligently practiced the piano. I loved playing the piano and looked forward to our lessons with our music teacher Mrs. Nixon. Like clockwork she used to come to the house with her developmentally delayed teenage daughter Annie in tow. With Mrs. Nixon's help I progressed in my lessons and dreamed of one day becoming a skilled musician. During high school I was thrilled to get the chance to play piano on a

Christmas album my school produced, and when I graduated from high school I received a scholarship for musical achievement and played the piano at my graduation.

As strong as my memories of Papa are, my memories of Grandmother Willie are faint and almost ethereal, but no less dear to me. Because my mother worked nights and my father and stepfather were often stationed away, it was Willie who spent a lot of time caring for us. Much of what I remember about Willie is emotional impressions. I have fleeting images and sounds of what she was like when she was alive. One of my earliest memories is of her letting me play with her beautiful long hair as she held me in her arms and tenderly rocked me to sleep by singing quietly in my ear. Her voice was almost a whisper, and I must have been all of three at the time, but to this day I distinctly remember the song, "I Come to the Garden Alone." Later she taught me the lyrics, and this song still has the power to move me and is a source of spiritual and emotional comfort. I take strength from its verses.

I can still picture what my grandmother Willie looked like. She was short and had a solid frame, but she was stunning to look at, with fair skin that made her look almost white. She had gorgeous green eyes and long straight hair that cascaded down her back, which I was enthralled with as a little girl. The texture was soft, and Willie would let me comb it as she rocked me slowly back and forth until I fell asleep. I was only five when she died suddenly of congestive heart failure. Her death left me feeling not really sure how to cope with the powerful sense of loss that I felt. I distinctly remember the morning she died—Papa was standing very still looking out the front door window and crying silently. He was always impeccably dressed and this morning was no exception, he had on a beige sweater, white shirt, tie, and a pair of crisply ironed pants. As I recall this memory, I am so overcome with grief, pain, and sadness that tears are streaming down my face. Even after all of these years the memory of that morning is still powerfully emotional for me.

Following her death, we had a series of live-in housekeepers from Juarez, and many of them were variously named Lupe and Maria. They cooked, cleaned house, taught us to speak Spanish, and in general, took care of us. They were very much a part of our family, I loved them very much, and I am still in touch with Maria, who I helped by sending money for her to finish school. Even though this was unusual back then, it made perfect sense to me because my mother worked full time, my grandfather was in his seventies, and my father and then later my stepfather were often stationed elsewhere. Living in the house where my grandmother died made my grandfather's grief too unbearable and so he decided it was time to move to California, and sold the house; as my Papa said, they had better schools and a chance at an education out there. It was 1960. Both of my mother's sisters were already living in California; Auntie Juanita was in Pacoima and Auntie Lois was in Oakland. When we moved to San Fernando, California, my mother got a job as a government insurance clerk.

The year I was 14 was one of turmoil, pain, and confusion; it was the year that my universe was turned upside down. The financial worries brought on by my stepfather Bill's lack of money management led to my mother's hospitalization for nervous anxiety. Meanwhile my sisters and I were at home with my grandfather, who by then was in his mid-eighties and getting senile. One night the phone rang at two o'clock in the morning, and the caller identified himself as James Lewis. He said that he was my father. He said he wanted to tell me and my sister Mildred how much he loved us and that he was going to send me a typewriter and buy me a red sports car for my junior high school graduation, which he promised to attend. I had no idea who this man was. Nothing he said made sense. There was no way he could be my father because the only father I had ever known was Garvin Tutt, an Army man and my mom's first husband. This man rambled on for hours, yet somehow he knew things about Mildred and me. I kept repeating over and over again to him that my mother was in the hospital. After that first call he continued to call for another three or four nights, and I was at a loss over what to do. I was the oldest child but I was still just a child myself. I was left on my own to deal with this completely baffling and shocking news; I had no adult to turn to for help, comfort, guidance, or answers to my questions.

When my mother was released from the hospital, I told her about the calls. She became hysterical because she had moved away from him in secret so that he couldn't find us. It was obvious that she was still terrified of him and even considered moving away again just to get away from him. What I didn't know at the time was that James Lewis had been telling me the truth, that he—not Garvin Tutt, who I for years had thought of as my father—was my biological father. It turned out that during World War II, my mother had left El Paso with the intention of moving to Washington, DC, to get a wartime job. Along the way, she stopped in Portsmouth, Virginia, where her older sister Juanita and brother-in-law Albert were living at the time. While there, she ended up getting a job and met James Henderson Lewis, who was a friend of Juanita's next door neighbor. He convinced her to stay in Portsmouth and marry him, which she did. James' mother Maude Ash Howell knew that her son was nothing but trouble, and later, after my parents were divorced, she told my mother that she would have advised my mother not to marry him had she been able to be alone with her without my father around.

After the divorce, my mom met and married Garvin Tutt, who legally adopted us, and is my sister Beverly's biological father. When he learned the story of my biological father, Garvin thought that my mother should tell my sister Mildred and me the truth about our real father and although my mother claims she did tell us the story, I don't remember her ever doing so. According to my mother, when I was about seven or eight, she took Mildred and me to a Dairy Queen and told us about our father James Lewis. Aside from my father's late night phone calls during my mother's hospital stay, I have only had contact with my biological father twice in my lifetime, once not long after my parents divorced when I was about two and the second time much later on, after Garvin had adopted Mildred and me. The first visit began with my grandmother Maude coming to the house to warn my mother about her son James' coming. To protect us, my mother left Mildred and me at home with my Auntie Juanita who was visiting my grandmother Maude and Papa, who was armed with a .45 caliber pistol. Let me tell you, he certainly was not going to put up with any trouble from a man who beat women. What my mother did that day took courage. She was frightened not just because he had repeatedly beaten her, but because he had threatened to kill her. She believed that he could and would kill her if given the chance.

The only other time we saw my father was when we were living in Berkeley. My mother took us to Aunt Lois' house in Oakland, and he visited us there while Garvin and my Uncle Melvin both stood guard to make sure nothing would happen. He wasn't allowed to come into the house because my mother was afraid he was going to kidnap us, and she was worried that if he got his hands on us he would try to force her to go back to him. My sister and I were told that he was a friend of my father's, strangely; I have no recollection of any of this meeting ever happening.

As odd as our only contact with him was in life, my father unceremoniously left my life for good just a few months after my mother returned from the hospital. We received a telegram from my grandmother Maude telling us of her son's death. Those bizarre nights all alone and talking to my father were, I truly believe, his attempt to reconcile with me because he was terminally ill and dying, and he knew that those late night calls were his last chance to speak with us. Despite everything he put my family through, it makes me sad that I never got a chance to know him. I know that all of this drama in my family and our confusing family tree may seem shocking to many people, but as my mother has always said about her husbands, they were not my stepfathers. Instead she said that "He is your daddy for now . . . sometimes things change." I have learned to live with my past and have tried to reconcile the reality of my family relations so that I am at peace in my own mind.

One of the most profoundly tragic events of my life occurred in August of 1964, and it shattered my world forever. The day started out normal enough, with Papa leaving the house in the morning but never coming back; it was as if he had disappeared into thin air. As the search for him continued, we received word two weeks later that his decomposed body was found under a Los Angeles freeway. We will never know for sure what happened to him, how his life ended, or why he was found where he was, but he was transported to El Paso for the funeral. What was so heart wrenching for me about his passing was that I was living in England at the time, and I tried desperately to get back to the States in time for his funeral. Back then the Red Cross had a program that gave financial assistance to family members who could not afford to travel out of town to attend a relative's funeral. I applied to them for financial assistance but my request was denied, and Mother thought making the trip back to the United States when I had just recently arrived in England didn't make sense. She encouraged me to stay with my husband. I wish now that I had made the trip anyway because I wasn't there when they buried my beloved Papa, and the agony of being so far away and the loss of someone who was so central in my life was the worst emotional pain I have ever known. I was so close to Papa that leaving him to move to England with my new husband Carl was one of the hardest things I have ever done. I remember that as I was leaving him to travel overseas, his goodbye was oddly discomforting because he made a comment to me about never seeing me again and emphasized that his job raising me was now done. At the time I didn't understand what he meant or give the comment any thought but I am sure he somehow saw the future. He died two months later.

By the time I was twenty, I had lived in England, been married and divorced, had two young boys, moved to northern California, and was living on public assistance. How I ended up on public assistance is a cautionary tale that we should all pay attention to, because it doesn't take much in our society or economy to fall through the cracks and become destitute. In my case I was broke, because although I took my ex-husband, Carl, to court several times, for whatever reasons, I never received steady child support. This is often the case with women and children living on welfare; it's not a matter of mothers not wanting to work as much as it is not having child support or enough child support to make ends meet. To compound matters, the district attorney wouldn't enforce the child support orders. I had to give my ex-husband pretty much every asset worth anything just to gain custody of the children. Because I was the one who had left Carl, who was a good husband and father, I think it was guilt that kept me from being more aggressive in pursuing child support. And it was this desperate situation that forced me to go on public assistance, a financial support that I needed to get back on my feet. I bought a home with the help of a section 235 HUD mortgage loan and got a scholarship, financial aid, and work-study money so I could go to college.

During this time, the personal issues I had confronted and the obstacles faced by women, children, and the poor served to further my resolve to work for peaceful solutions to conflict and improve or create safety nets for people who are struggling. My work as a politician on the state and national level reflects the hard lessons I have learned and my commitment to make things better for others. For example, in 1992, after I was elected to the California Assembly, then Gov. Pete Wilson said he wanted to cut welfare benefits by 25 percent and went on to say that recipients would simply "have less for a six-pack of beer." Well, when he said this, I took him on with a vengeance. I remembered those days sitting at the welfare office at 401 Broadway trying to get food stamps and MediCal to feed my kids and keep them healthy. The disdain and disrespect with which I was treated was demoralizing, and all I wanted to do was survive and get through school so I could raise my children in a respectful manner. Being on welfare was a humiliating experience but it was also enlightening because I now know firsthand how stressful and frightening it is to think that you can't meet your family's basic needs of food, clothing, and shelter in a wealthy country with un-limited resources at its disposal. We don't have many mechanisms to help people become self-reliant, and we also make the welfare system adversarial. Add the problems created by economic insta-bility and the pressures one encounters just trying to eke out a liv-ing, and it's almost impossible for a person to achieve his or her full potential.

Hardship and struggle have taught me many things, probably be-cause I was forced to learn how to restructure my value system. From life's lessons I have learned that monetary gain is nothing compared to love, understanding, commitment, peak experiences, and true human relationships. As a result of my own degrading encounter with the welfare system, I feel I am better equipped to understand some of the basic evils of society and how psychologically sick and frustrated people become when the very institutions and safety nets that are set up to help them do little to address their long-term needs and goals. The people whom welfare was meant to help were not broken; the inadequate welfare programs were. When I served in the California Legislature, I refused to vote for any cuts to pro-grams and funding that provided assistance to women with children, to senior citizens, the disabled, and for general assistance, and I wrote California's first Violence Against Women Act.

As a co-chair of the conference committee on the Personal Re-sponsibility and Work Opportunity Reconciliation Act of 1996, better known as the "Welfare Reform Bill," I made sure that the bill contained provisions for increased funding for child care, drug and alcohol treatment programs, and programs and resources designed to help women fleeing domestic violence. Unfortunately, as hard as I worked to make this bill better, in the end I was forced to vote against it. Why? Because the law required women drop out of college to receive public assistance and barred anyone ever convicted of a drug offense from receiving public assistance or food stamps, for life. It provided no second chance for people who need a safety net or "a bridge over troubled water." I am not totally naïve and realize that there are some people who run scams on the system, and I agree that they need to be dealt with appropriately. That being said, the majority of people who benefited from welfare were poor women and children who never wanted to be on welfare in the first place; what these women genuinely wanted was to be able to fend for themselves. Welfare recipients want the same things that most Americans do. They want the opportunity to go to school, get trained, get a job, and take care of their families and to do so with dignity. Many people have a negative view of those receiving welfare. It's as if the women who receive welfare are inherently flawed or defective human beings. As a former welfare recipient, when I hear other legislators demean welfare recipients, I make a point of reminding them that they are talking about me too.

It has often been said the foundation for the rest of your life is formed in the early years of childhood, and I believe this as well. Untold numbers of people have faced, and continue to face, far greater adversities than I have ever known. Truly, I have been blessed. I have benefited from a family who loved me and provided for me. I have gotten a good education, and despite the painful lessons I have learned, each life experience has made me into the woman I am today. Just knowing that my constituents may be going through some of the same difficulties I did makes me want to work harder for the people in my district and throughout the country.

I have taken a strong stand on the issue of domestic violence and know how damaging to a child's future it can be. It's not easy to recognize and deal with the legacy of patterns of family violence but, ultimately, violence against women is also an insidious form of child abuse. It subjects impressionable children to a repetitive cycle of abuse and violence that can continue for generations. By watching men beat their mothers, boys learn that it is okay to use violence to resolve conflict, they learn that women deserve to be hit. It normalizes violence, making it more likely that boys who grow up in violent homes will become abusers as adults. When girls see their mothers beaten or psychologically badgered, it teaches them that they have no right to live without fearing that their loved ones will be violent, that they have no voice or control over their lives, that they cannot stand up for themselves, and that if a man hits them, they must have done something wrong to deserve it.

One of the reasons I wrote this book is because I believe God wants us to be strong, not fragile, and I want to be a living example and show that people can triumph over adversity. If people don't face head-on the root cause of their challenges, they are doomed to repeat their mistakes and face these same challenges over and over again. This is a daily struggle for me, but I am proud of my success and I believe my challenges have given me a foundation for conquering the cycle of abuse and its patterns that my mother endured—and as you will learn later, even in my adult life. I have been blessed with two sons with whom I believe I have broken the pattern of violence and abuse. Even while I continue to fight some battles on my own, they are my personal legacy and are in stable healthy marriages, and I know they have wonderful children. It is my faith in God and in doing His work that gives me strength, and I know that if I believe in Him I can accomplish anything.

Chapter Two

Religion without humanity is very poor human stuff.

—Sojourner Truth

Looking back now, I realize that much of my childhood in El Paso was centered on faith and trying to do God's will. My grandfather was deeply religious and passed down his spiritual convictions to his daughters and granddaughters. In some ways, I think I am still living out my childhood, and I have an abiding faith in God and a conviction that the Bible can guide us to do the Lord's will and live righteously. My faith has had a profound effect in my personal and professional life, and I try to follow the words of Proverbs 3:5: "Trust in the LORD with all thine heart; and lean not unto thine own understanding."

When I was a girl living with Papa seven days out of the week, many of our social activities and other obligations were somehow related to the Church. In our house, religious diversity was a way of life, and we practiced several Christian faiths—my mother belonged to the United Methodist Church, my grandfather was a member of the African Methodist Episcopal Church, and my sisters and I attended St. Joseph's, a private Roman Catholic school where we had daily Bible study, were taught the catechism, and attended Mass five days a week. I have strong memories of attending both my mother and Papa's church every Sunday which wasn't easy. Just keeping the schedules clear in our minds was difficult, let alone the time commitment involved in going to two churches every Sunday. Saturdays were also busy, and we often sang at Catholic weddings or funerals and attended our Eastern Star Lodge meetings. It turns out that we were not the only St. Joseph's students worshipping at more than one church because a year or two before we moved from Texas to California, another black girl, Bertha, who was an Army brat like us, enrolled in our school. One Sunday, we went to Papa's church, and for reasons we were terrified to contemplate, she was there too. Mildred and I were really worried she was going to tell the nuns we weren't at a Catholic church on Sunday, but Bertha kept our secret and never said anything.

Our school was run by the Order of the Sisters of Loretto, and I was a student there from first through eighth grades. My sisters and I attended school there because the public schools in El Paso were segregated when we started school, and sending all three of us to private school was not in our budget. Besides, my mother thought we could benefit from the strict discipline and academic excellence the Sisters were known for. This was long enough ago now, that the Sisters wore the traditional habits that many associate with religious communities: the long black robes, white collar, and long black- and white-framed wimple that completely hid their hair. Sometimes Mildred and I wondered if they had hair at all. My teachers were genuinely interested in helping me learn the subjects, which included the standard subjects taught in any school along with daily Bible study and catechism. The Sisters of Loretto were dedicated and had deeply held convictions about the righteousness of their calling. They prayed the rosary and went to Mass every day, as we all did. The Sisters were strong women. I admired them, so much in fact that at one point I seriously considered joining their order, although I was intimidated by their strict traditional habit.

With their help, I learned the Eight Beatitudes of Jesus Christ that were given in the Sermon on the Mount as recorded in the Gospel of Matthew 5:3–10. In the Beatitudes, Jesus offers a way of life that promises life ever after in the kingdom of heaven. When He handed down the Beatitudes, they were the culmination of His teachings and were the values of simple humble people who, without fanfare or accolade, know and serve their God, whatever the cost, including suffering and ridicule. Jesus spoke of brotherly love, humility, and charity, and He taught the transformation of the inner self. Many people do not truly grasp these values because to live by them requires great sacrifice. For me, however, these sacred words provided a foundation for the values that guide my religious and public service.

> Blessed are the poor in spirit, for theirs is the kingdom of heaven.
> Blessed are they who mourn, for they shall be comforted.
> Blessed are the meek, for they shall inherit the earth.
> Blessed are they who hunger and thirst for righteousness, for they shall be satisfied.
> Blessed are the merciful, for they shall obtain mercy.
> Blessed are the pure of heart, for they shall see God.
> Blessed are the peacemakers, for they shall be called children of God.
> Blessed are they who are persecuted for the sake of righteousness, for theirs is the kingdom of heaven.

As a child, I was introverted and insecure, and my sisters and I being one of the few black students at St. Joseph's made me even more self-conscious. There was no such thing as a black history curriculum back then, and when slavery was discussed, we had the shared experience of everyone turning and looking at us as the modern repository for history. Nonetheless, I enjoyed school and particularly liked English, Religion, and Logic, which were taught by Monsignor Buchanan. I also loved my singing lessons and was encouraged to sing more by my teacher, the Monsignor's sister, the Irish-American Julia, who later as a young woman wrote me letters to help me work through my anger at how black people were treated in America. Although I disliked math, it fortunately didn't keep me from being a good student. I never got anything other than As and Bs, and I entered and won a lot of spelling bees. In English class we were taught how to diagram sentences, something that none of my friends in my neighborhood were learning at their school. I loved English.

While attending St. Joseph's, the holy sisters were supportive of my family's Protestant faith, and although they acknowledged and accepted us as Methodists, we were forbidden to take holy communion at Mass because we had not been confirmed in the Roman Catholic Church, a fact which greatly troubled me. I strongly believed then in the teachings of the Catholic Church, and my inability to take holy communion with the rest of the children was just one more thing that made my sisters and me different from the other students. When I turned ten and reached the age of consent under the Church's rules regarding the conversion of non-Catholics, my mother agreed to let me get baptized as a Roman Catholic and make my first communion.

My mother firmly believes that, "When you leave one church, you go to another. There's really no difference. Religion is religion. The Bible is the Bible," so she had no problem with my converting to Catholicism. She, however, had no intention of becoming a Catholic because while studying Catholicism, a priest flirted with her. She is proud that faith was a large part of my development, although she jokes that while my sisters and I may have been angels at school, we were devils at home. Receiving my first communion was one of the happiest times of my life because I was finally a part of the Church that was educating me and because my sister Mildred made hers the same day. Since the other children in my school had received this sacrament when they were seven, we were the only ones to do so that day. My mother and stepfather, Bill Massey, were there, along with my mother's good friends, Harry B. Jackson and James Jackson, who were my godparents. I wore an abstract pat-terned, silky blue and green, short sleeved, v-necked dress I made myself. My mother's attention to our spiritual education was very influential but she also paid close attention to raising us as accom-plished well-rounded girls and she sacrificed a lot so she could pay for us to have a normal middle-class upbringing.

Despite my faith and religious education, I became sexually ac-tive a few years after we moved to California. I attended public school for the first time, and the pressures and environment there were very different from my previous school experience. Although my sexual activity might seem contradictory to my religious devo-tion and my family's faith, I still considered myself a devout Catholic and at the time I didn't give the contradiction much thought. I felt I was being consistent because I supported the Church's position on medical contraception, and believed the rhythm method was effective. That conclusion led inevitably to my getting pregnant in November of 1962 at the age of 16, not exactly a propitious moment for me as I had just been elected San Fer-nando High School's first black cheerleader and the news of my pregnancy was devastating to me.

I had only been dating Carl for about a year, and I desperately wanted to finish high school. I knew that education was an important part of living a successful life and to go to college I would need an excellent education. My mother never approved of my boyfriend who was three or four years older than I and already in college. She always said that Carl could stare right through anyone. To a love-struck teenager, all that mattered was that I loved him, and I thought that the only way to express that love was by going to bed with him. I was certain that this was the ultimate expression of my feelings and yet knew nothing about conception, contraception, and how easy it was to get pregnant. As a result of my own refusal to think things through, and my lack of sex education, I was living a nightmare that also posed extremely difficult moral and ethical dilemmas for me and my religious beliefs. An abortion was out of the question, but so was the thought of dropping out of school to become a full-time mother at the age of 16. I was scared and unsure what to do and also felt guilty about my sexual activity, about letting down my teachers, my school, my family, and, yes, my race.

I found myself going to confession almost every Saturday to try to assuage some of my guilt and even a long span of years has not diminished this overpowering sense of guilt. I wondered why God had given me what seemed to be such an insurmountable challenge. For guidance, I read the Bible and drew comfort from 2 Corinthians 2:9 which says, "For to this end also did I write, that I might know the proof of you, whether ye be obedient in all things." It was with God's help and His guidance that my mother was able to devise a plan that would prevent my public humiliation at school and still let me marry the man I loved. I would marry Carl, keep my marriage and baby a secret until I graduated from high school, and I would continue to live at home. Carl joined the Air Force and was stationed at Castle AFB. Hopefully, I would have the baby when school was out.

Fortunately for us, our plan was going along smoothly, and I married Carl in March. We had our wedding at a minister's house in Bakersfield, and the service was held in his small cluttered dining room. For such a small space it was piled high with newspapers and an array of clothing. The scene was not romantic or uplifting seeing as how the minister's shirt was hanging out of his pants as he read us our vows; he seemed as indifferent to us and our marriage as he was about his personal grooming and the cleanliness of his home. But he was definitely interested in the fifty dollars we paid him to perform the ceremony. Due to the circumstances, the wedding party was small and included Carl's mother as well as my mother, my sisters, and my Aunt Juanita.

I went back to school as though nothing had happened. My baby was due in August, and I was lucky to have the luxury of time that would allow me to give birth away from prying and mocking eyes at school. I looked forward to going back to school in September, with no one the wiser, but God had other plans for me. A few weeks after my marriage, at the beginning of Easter school vacation, I had a spontaneous miscarriage. My water broke after I got up one Saturday morning, and mother put me into the car and we drove to Sun Valley Hospital. It was there that my three and a half month long pregnancy ordeal abruptly ended. I was very sad, but I was also relieved that I wouldn't have to juggle being a cheerleader, high school student, and young wife and mother. The timing of my miscarriage also gave me the private time I needed to adjust to my loss because it happened at the beginning of a week off from school and gave me time to recuperate both mentally and physically.

Because I was no longer pregnant, my mother saw no reason why Carl and I should continue to be married, and she encouraged me to annul my marriage, but I adamantly refused. As a devout Catholic at that time, I believed I was married for life, and I loved my husband with all of the passion a teenager has. Despite my pregnancy and other regrettable errors I've made in my life, I continue to have faith in God's forgiveness and believe in His will. I believe that He led me in the 1970s to attend the Church for Today in

Berkeley led by the Pastor Rev. Dr. W. Hazaiah Williams. An inspiring and well-educated theologian who had earned his master's degree in theology from Boston University, Rev. Williams' approach was so different in that he was a nondenominational minister and a brilliant progressive. He was a pillar of resolve, and he supported me and strengthened my conviction that I should make a lifelong commitment to public service. Hazaiah was a true revolutionary who interpreted the Bible and the teachings of Jesus Christ, as well as other prophets whose works he often used in his sermons, in a deeply profound way. His sermons often emphasized the concept that Jesus was a revolutionary who would not accept the status quo and that if we are true Christians, our life and work is about taking on a system fraught with racism, sexism, injustice, and oppression and bringing about change.

Hazaiah did not believe that God was punitive, but saw Him as someone who had sent Jesus Christ to this earth to help the poor and the disadvantaged and to change society from being oppressive to being committed to justice and peace. The following excerpt is from one of my favorite sermons of his, "Searching the Ground of My Intention," which is an example of the profound insight he had about the partnership between faith and service, a tenet that has become a cornerstone in my life.

I want to tell you a story. This scene takes place someplace in Heaven. Jesus, after being crucified, had gone to God to report, and God said to him, "You failed to let them know about my ways." Jesus said, "No, Father, they know." "But you failed to make them want it." He said, "No, they wanted it, but they were fearful of wanting it so much lest that wanting should destroy them, so they crucified me." "But you failed to teach them that they could contain it, that they could live it, and you failed to teach them that my perfection was livable." "Yes, Father, in the moment they crucified me, I did fail; but the manner, the manner of my Life, will haunt them until they come to Thee." Wanting is nothing in this business that we are talking about today—nothing. I want to be holy. I want to be a Christian. Wanting is just the starting point, if even that. Doing is the next step, and that is not even enough.

Hazaiah was a man who made things happen and his love of God's music led him to found "Today's Artists," a groundbreaking major concert series that was the first of its kind in the country. His leadership and talents have been widely recognized in America and when he started this concert series, he became the first African American impresario of this kind of musical performance, holding concerts at Carnegie Hall in New York City and in San Francisco. While still in college, I helped him establish the National Black Church Arts Program and learned how to involve the community in classical music appreciation. He paid a friend and me $250 apiece each month to do this. Hazaiah was a true Renaissance man who I loved deeply for many reasons, and we were close friends. At one point I even had a crush on him. With Hazaiah's death in 1999, the world lost a great leader and a true follower of the teachings of Jesus, and I lost a dear friend. Hazaiah was instrumental in my spiritual growth and introduced me to other religious leaders, teachers, writers, and thinkers, such as the prolific Dr. Howard Thurman, whom I met at Hazaiah's house and the fireside chats with Dr. Thurman influenced me deeply. Dr. Thurman was the author of twenty books on ethical and cultural criticism, the most famous of which was *Jesus and the Disinherited*, a book which deeply influenced Martin Luther King, Jr. and other leaders of the civil rights movement.

I joined Allen Temple Baptist Church in Oakland, and this church for me has become a place of community and fellowship. It is a sanctuary where I can join other African Americans. Allen Temple Baptist Church is a place where as African Americans we can take pride in our culture and celebrate our distinct history. As a member of this church I have helped organize visits of black leaders who have addressed the concerns of African Americans. These leaders have exposed the members of our church to the rich diversity of our people. One special voice that offered another perspective on our place in the world as people of faith, change, and brotherly love was Archbishop Desmond Tutu, whose visit to northern California I was instrumental in making possible. During his tour he came to Allen Temple and spoke eloquently about the need for understanding. During his sermon he said, "We are different so that we can know our need of one another, for no one is ultimately self-sufficient. A completely self-sufficient person would be subhuman." His words remain in my heart to this day, for it was through these words that I got to know The Rev. Dr. J. Alfred Smith, Sr. and the Allen Temple Church even better. The first time I heard Pastor Smith preach, something came over me, a very spiritual and profound feeling that drew me there and compelled me to become a member.

Pastor Smith has become a spiritual mentor I rely on, and I thank God for individuals like him who stand in the gap, fighting shoulder-to-shoulder for social justice. He is an African American of faith who has never forgotten his roots or his culture; his prayers with and for me helped me with my decision to vote against the 9/11 resolution. He continues to provide wise counsel and spiritual support and gives me and others a platform to speak at church. He is a powerful community leader and has always endorsed me in my many political campaigns. In addition, Pastor Smith encourages me to write about, reflect on, and interpret the spiritual dimensions of my life. Pastor Smith also sees what I do not, and he helps me understand the path that I am on. His church has honored me with awards and has graciously shown its support and appreciation of my work. Allen Temple Baptist Church has become part of my extended family. Pastor Smith's son, Rev. J. Alfred Smith, Jr., a prolific preacher and teacher, has also been a friend and confidant. I will never forget my uncertainty about traveling to Israel in the early 1990s. Rev. Smith and Pastor Smith both took me to lunch and convinced me my trip to Israel was important because they both knew that one day I would have to address the issues of peace in the Middle East. Somehow they knew that this visit to the Holy Land would have a profound impact on me spiritually and politically and that I needed to better understand the complexity of the necessity for Israel's security and for Palestinian justice. Now years later, serving in the House of Representatives and after two visits to Israel, their prophetic insights have become clear to me.

During each important era in my life I have had the benefit of help and intercession from religious and spiritual guides such as the Sisters of Loretto, Rev. Williams, Pastor Smith, and many others. They have each taught me how God will help me cope with enormous dangers, toils, and snares. For example, in the early 1990s when I was a member of the California Assembly, I led a delegation to West Africa. We visited Ghana and had a remarkable visit with then President Jerry Rawlings and his wife at their home on the Volta River. We spent Easter Sunday with Isaac Hayes and Dionne Warwick on a boat ride up the river with President Rawlings and his wife. When we departed Ghana on a small plane, one engine failed. Then it seemed like the second engine went dead, and we literally glided back to the airport. As the plane floated quietly through the air, my friends were praying and leaning forward to brace ourselves for a crash landing, and yet, as terrifying as this was, we somehow knew we would be okay. The Ghanaian pilots flying the plane were skilled experienced pilots so all I could do was trust in the Lord. Later, I was shaken when I found out just how dangerous our flight really had been and that we almost didn't make it. This was not the first or last time that I put my faith and destiny into the hands of the Lord, and over the years I have had to trust in Him many times in my public life like in the 1980s when I was traveling in Grenada amid assassination attempts of government officials, or in southern Lebanon during a visit to the refugee camps in Sidon and Tyre when I nearly stepped on a cluster bomb, or sitting in the Capitol that fateful morning of September 11th and being told to evacuate Washington because a plane might be coming to hit the Capitol or the White House, or being faced with a barrage of death threats and harassing e-mails and phone calls for voting against giving the Bush administration the authorization to go to war. In each instance I have felt the hand of God intervene. Out of suffering and hard times, I have learned God puts detours in our way to remind us who is in the driver's seat. Time and again, I return to one of my favorite scriptures to help me through these moments, Ephesians 6:13–18:

> Therefore put on the full armor of God, so that when the day of evil comes, you may be able to stand your ground and after you have done everything to stand. Stand firm then, with the belt of truth buckled around your waist, with the breastplate of righteousness in place, and with your feet fitted with the readiness that comes from the gospel of peace. In addition to all this, take up the shield of faith, with which you can extinguish all the flaming arrows of the evil one. Take the helmet of salvation and the sword of the Spirit, which is the word of God. And pray in the Spirit on all occasions with all kinds of prayers and requests. With this in mind, be alert and always keep on praying for all the saints.

Every step along the way, I believe God has presented me with a series of tests: tests of faith and tests that prepared me for the hard road that lay ahead. My faith in God and the teachings of Jesus Christ, the guidance of my religious mentors, my experiences as a teenager and young adult, a lifetime facing challenges have all influenced my desire to help young girls build their self-esteem and surmount the challenges of young adulthood. All of these parts of my journey have led me to work for change and remind me that the unseen hand of God is always present. My desire to bring about change along with my training as a social worker have driven a lot of my legislative and political work. I draw strength from power of the Word and am willing to testify to my firsthand knowledge of the trauma of unwanted and early pregnancy and the consequences that result from a lack of sex education. I know too many teenage girls who don't have family support, lack access to community resources, or don't know how to exercise their options. Maybe I'm still trying to overcome the guilt of my youthful indiscretions by trying to help others. So I work on a range of programs that give young girls, women, and their families options that offer real-world solutions. One area that I am active in is the repeal of the so-called "abstinence-only" policy that was introduced during the Clinton administration. This is a policy that sadly has not only proven ineffective in preventing teen pregnancy but also led to the spread of sexually transmitted diseases, or STDs.

The insistence on "abstinence-only" policies led Congress in 1996 to add a provision to the Personal Responsibility and Work Opportunity Reconciliation Act, commonly referred to as the "Welfare Reform Act." This provision appropriated $250 million over five years for state initiatives that promoted sexual abstinence outside of marriage as the *only* acceptable standard of sexual behavior for young people. For the first five years of the initiative, every state except California participated. My state had experimented with its own "abstinence-only" initiative in the early 1990s, but this program was terminated in February 1996 when an evaluation deemed it ineffective. From 1998 to 2003, almost a half billion dollars in state and federal funds were allocated to support the "abstinence-only" initiative. A report detailing the results of the federally funded evaluation of select Title V programs was due in 2006, but was delayed and finally completed in April 2007. The independent research firm, Mathematica Policy Research, Inc. released a study commissioned by the U.S. Department of Health and Human Services concluding that students in "abstinence-only" programs are no more likely to abstain from sex, delay initiation of sex, or have fewer sexual partners than students who did not participate. Moreover, at least 13 states have evaluated their federally funded "abstinence-only" programs and not one found a positive long term impact. In fact, in some cases young people who participated in the programs actually increased their sexual activity. Many medical and public health organizations including the National Academy of Sciences' Institute of Medicine have criticized the federal government's investment of hundreds of millions of dollars in the programs as "poor fiscal and public health policy."

I believe this policy was ineffective and put more lives at risk by telling people to abstain without giving them information about how to protect themselves from disease and unwanted pregnancy if they have sex. I believe this policy isolated us then and continues to isolate us now from the global community. Our youth would be better served with a comprehensive sex education policy, and so in March 2007, Rep. Christopher Shays (R-CT), Sen. Frank R. Lautenberg (D-NJ), and I introduced HR 2553, the Responsible Education About Life (REAL) Act, a bill that would have authorized federal funding for states to offer comprehensive and medically accurate sex education in their schools. We need to get real about sex education. We should be teaching young people about abstinence, but that doesn't mean holding back information that can save lives and prevent the spread of sexually transmitted diseases and unwanted pregnancies. It's time to get REAL about protecting our young people. It is time to get REAL about providing our young people with the tools they need to stop unwanted pregnancies and fight HIV/AIDS and other deadly diseases. Instead of "abstinence-only," we are proposing "abstinence-plus." Research has clearly shown that the most effective sexual education programs include both a focus on delaying sexual behavior and providing information on how sexually active young people can protect themselves. It has been proven that teenagers who are in programs that include discussion of both options are more likely to delay sexual activity and to use contraceptives when they do become sexually active.

Tied to the failure of the "abstinence-only" approach are the short-sighted and oppressive measures related to abortion rights, particularly the Global Gag Rule which I worked to repeal. This rule was reinstated by President George W. Bush on his first day in office in January 2001 amid accusations that the United Nations Population Fund, which the United States is a substantial contributor to, was involved in subsidizing forced abortions and coerced sterilizations in China. Officially termed the Mexico City Policy, the Global Gag Rule says that no U.S. family planning assistance can be provided to foreign NGOs that use funding to: perform abortions in cases other than a threat to the woman's life, rape, or incest; provide counseling and referral for abortion; or lobby to make abortion legal or more available in their country. This order also undercut efforts by family planning groups to help restrain population growth, limit unwanted pregnancies, and stem the spread of HIV/AIDS and other sexually transmitted diseases. Furthermore, one day I would like to repeal the Hyde Amendment, which denies federal funding for safe abortions for women who are poor or have low incomes. I have always believed that if an attempt to institutionalize the Mexico City Policy were implemented here in the United States, it would be deemed unconstitutional. We should not impose unfair, dangerous provisions like this on women in other nations.

The first congressional vote to overturn Bush's Executive Order would have included my amendment to help foreign nations with family planning services, but it failed by a 218–210 vote in May 2001. It lacked the necessary votes because some Republican members and a few Democrats insisted my amendment was a covert way of providing abortion funding, but they were wrong. My amendment was not about abortion. Not one single penny of UN money in the program would have gone for abortions. My provision also stated that in the future, the president could cut off funds to the UN agency if it were shown that it directly participated in providing abortions or other banned activities. Until this was overturned almost two years later to the day, the cutoff of U.S. funds led to an estimated 552,000 abortions being performed, many of them unsafe, and one million women being forced into having unwanted pregnancies because they lost access to birth control devices and counseling. In all, 2.7 million women lost access to modern contraception.

My experiences as a young, married mother have led me to emphasize economic independence and political empowerment for women and their children, and in 1999, I supported the Fathers Count Act which gives grants to state agencies and nonprofit groups, including faith-based institutions to teach parenting skills to poor, noncustodial fathers and to enhance their employability so they can meet child support obligations. Other services would have included anger management training, family planning information, tips on relationship skills, and money management techniques. If we want to end the epidemic of fatherless families headed by teenage mothers living on the edge of financial and social destitution, this kind of program should encourage fathers to spend more time visiting their children and play a larger role in their children's lives.

As much as I am a woman of faith, I have generally opposed the Bush administration's faith-based initiatives because I believed that choosing to oppose charitable choice for faith-based organizations is to oppose neither charity nor choice. Both are absolutely essential to our values and traditions. In 2001, the House of Representatives passed the Community Solutions Act, a bill that allowed federal funding of church-run social programs that also included worship and religious activities. This bill essentially nullified the requirement that nonprofits keep social service programs separate from activities of worship. I opposed this initiative because I oppose government intrusion into our houses of worship, the corrosion of fundamental constitutional principles, and the use of taxpayer dollars to fund discrimination. I believe strongly in the separation of church and state and do not believe in pushing government money directly into church coffers. I support the tax exemptions for churches but I don't believe that tax dollars should be used to support institutions that are legally allowed to discriminate based on a person's religion.

For example, the Charitable Choice Initiative allows organizations to refuse to hire Jews, Catholics, Muslims, African American Baptists, or anyone if the job candidate's religion is not in line with the organization's religious policies and practices. This religious organization may receive federal funding and all the while be allowed to discriminate on the basis of religion—the very form of religious discrimination that our Constitution prohibits. The Charitable Choice Initiative specified that faith-based organizations cannot be excluded from the competition for federal funds simply because they are religious. This law provided that faith-based organizations that received federal funds must serve all eligible participants regardless of their religious beliefs but allowed them to carry out their missions consistent with their beliefs and maintain a religious environment in their community service facilities. This gave faith-based organizations that received federal funding the right to hire and fire employees based solely on religion. Thus if an employee's beliefs contradict those of the employer, that individual has no protections under federal employment law. I believe the federal government should provide aid to faith-based organizations that are active in the community but not at the cost of an employee's personal liberties or civil rights. Places of worship which have nonprofit 501(c)(3) organizations should definitely be able to receive federal funds.

Often, it's our faith that leads many of us into community service, and faith-based organizations do enormous good in our communities, in our country, and across the world. Nonprofit religious organizations should be supported with increased funding and technical assistance but, unfortunately, this bill did not provide one cent of funding for services of any kind. It however established a devastating legal precedent of sanctioning federally funded discrimination and the abrogation of civil rights laws. Currently, I am a member of Speaker Nancy Pelosi's Faith-Based Task Force, chaired by our democratic whip Jim Clyburn (D-SC), and the Congressional Black Caucus Faith-Based Task Force. I work with churches and the nonprofit organizations they sponsor. Because the Community Solutions Act never really achieved its goals and many churches have opted not to receive funding, I help churches and their social service programs by assisting them in getting federal funding by writing letters of support for their work in combating HIV/AIDS and in providing affordable housing. In the black community, the Church is a powerful symbol of strength, unity, and family, and it plays an important role in every part of life in the communities they serve.

I work closely with black churches on voter education, registration, and get-out-the-vote efforts because access to the corridors of power are essential to empowering black communities and bringing about change. To facilitate this two-way communication I am a frequent guest speaker at many churches. As African Americans we must make our voices heard, and Congress must know what issues are important to us as a people whose votes count. When I addressed a group of more than 200 faith leaders who performed civil disobedience on Capitol Hill to protest cuts in Medicaid, student loans, and food stamps, I encouraged them to call for a moral budget and I said, "Who better than you, who serve on the front lines, who feed the hungry, who clothe the naked, who house the homeless, to tell Congress about the impact of this immoral budget on our families and our communities. You recognize that the priorities reflected in our budget are not a partisan issue, but an issue of who we are as a nation, and what our values are. We know that the budget Congress is considering is, quite frankly, immoral, and it does not reflect our traditional American values. As a nation, we believe in equality, and opportunity, but belief, in and of itself, is not enough. We must work to make it so." I quoted James 2:14–17:

> What good is it, my brothers, if a man claims to have faith but has no deeds? Can such faith save him? Suppose a brother or sister is without clothes and daily food. If one of you says to him "go, I wish you well; keep warm and well fed," but does nothing about his physical needs, what good is it? In the same way, faith by itself, if it is not accompanied by action, is dead.

In my speeches I always emphasize that I rely on God to help get me through difficult times because although He gives us burdens, He also blesses us with unexpected joy—a lesson made clear to me shortly before I turned 60. I had traveled to the lovely town of Taos, New Mexico, to spend a couple of days in reflection. While driving along scenic roads, I followed the map I had with me and thought I knew where I was going, but I kept getting lost. As chance would have it, had I not gotten lost, I never would have had to make the detours I did, I never would have met the wonderful people I did, I would have missed going to amazing art galleries, and I never would have seen the beautiful pueblo homes that are part of this magical place. I was simply lucky enough to stumble across these treasures in spite of myself. Again He made my path straight and proved to me that leaning on my understanding alone just did not work. I believe that if you don't try to program, map out, and plan each mile of your life's road, if you let God's will be done and if you listen to His voice, you will follow what most people call their instincts, but what I believe are whispers from God pulling you in His direction. If you take the time to listen, you will experience the wonders of God and the awesome possibilities and opportunities He has in store for you. You will know that the rocks on the road are there to strengthen you, and you will know exactly what His will is for you.

❧

Chapter Three

You don't fight racism with racism, the best way to fight racism is with solidarity.

—Bobby Seale

The 1970s were a complicated time for me, and it was a time of discovery and ambivalence with many rocks and bumps along the road. At the time I was attending Mills College in Oakland, California. It is the second oldest women's school in the country. Mills College is a wonderful institution, and I tried to get as much from the college experience as possible and became active in a range of campus activities. My marriage to Carl had ended in divorce, and I knew that if I was going to make a successful future for my boys and me, I needed to get a college degree. I was given the time and freedom to pursue this goal by my in-laws, Peggy and Carl Lee, both of whom were kind and loving grandparents to my two boys. They lived on a farm in Texas and were able to take care of my boys for a couple of years so that I could go to school full time and fully dedicate myself to my degree. If they had not cared for Tony and Craig during this transition I would not have been able to finish my education and get my head together. Without their love and help, I probably wouldn't have made it. As it turned out, it was especially fortuitous that my sons were with their grandparents while I was at Mills because following my divorce I began to get involved in a toxic and abusive personal relationship that evolved into a repetitive pattern of physical and emotional domestic violence.

Despite the fact that my private life was a shambles, I was able to get more involved at school and pursued interests such as the Black Student Union (BSU) and eventually became president of the BSU. I also joined the Church for Today, and I became active in the progressive Black Panther Party, which is how I met founding members Huey Newton and Bobby Seale, as well as Elaine Brown, who became the head of the Party during the mid-1970s. As a budding student activist, I became involved with the Panther's revolutionary work, and these experiences and my interaction with people who were resolved to work for change helped me overcome the tremendous pain and depression I was experiencing. They gave me the confidence to move ahead with my life.

There has been a lot written about the Black Panther Party, its leaders, and its tactics and mission. When Huey and Bobby founded the Party in 1966 it had a core membership of about 40 people, including Eldridge Cleaver, author of *Soul On Ice*; Kathleen Cleaver who was its earliest female leader; Elaine Brown; and Angela Davis, the noted African American member of the Communist Party. A formal process for becoming a Black Panther Party member was developed but the organization also had a cadre of people called "community workers," and I was one of those during the early to mid-1970s. As a community worker, I had access to "mainstream" people and places Party members didn't because they were oftentimes seen as too radical. I could help raise money for the Party's various programs from private foundations and other resources while some of the more outspoken Party members simply never could have gotten access. I also used my organizational and fund-raising skills to help implement *The Ten-Point Program*, and by maximizing my credibility I was able to facilitate a lot of dialogue. This helped diffuse some of the middle-class folks' suspicions about the Party. For example, in an attempt to change the image of the Black Panther Party, Bobby Seale ran for mayor of Oakland in 1973, forcing a run-off with Republican incumbent Mayor John Reading. I was Bobby's fund-raising coordinator and raised money from a variety of middle-income individuals who were convinced that Bobby should be the candidate to support. Unfortunately, Bobby lost to Reading by 70 percent, but his strong showing proved how powerful a voice both he and the Party had become.

The principles of the Black Panther Party are stated in *The Ten-Point Program*, which was written by Huey and Bobby while Huey was attending law school at night and Bobby was working at the North Oakland Neighborhood Anti-Poverty Center. Based on his experiences there, and his exposure to the problems associated with poverty and the more traditional solutions, Bobby felt that more revolutionary ideas were needed. This desire for a more radical ideology was reflected in *The Ten-Point Program* of what we wanted and what we believed. This manifesto outlined the Party's goals which included: more equity in land ownership, food distribution, education, clothing, health care, justice and peace, and various ways to achieve them. Although *The Ten-Point Program* is often accused of being heavily influenced by Karl Marx's *The Communist Manifesto*, Bobby said the Party was based completely on study and research of African and African American struggles and that neither he nor Huey had read any of Marx's work before they wrote it.

So who were these new leaders who inspired so many young black people during the 1960s and 1970s? In reality they were a talented group of brilliant thinkers and organizers who were each accomplished in their own right and who believed passionately in righting the wrongs of our society. Huey was known as "the servant" and was an introverted, light-skinned black man who was not very tall—maybe five-foot-eight or nine, but he was muscular from all of the weight lifting he had done while in jail. He was also very tough and had a "street side" to his nature. Yet, despite his roughness, my mother really liked him and thought he was a gentleman. Huey could be intense, and sometimes when he looked at you, it felt as if his eyes were boring directly into you. He was a ball of energy and moved around a lot. He just couldn't sit still for any length of time and was an interesting combination of intensity and fastidiousness, and he was compulsive about cleanliness—he brushed his teeth several times a day and always insisted everything be in order. This attention to minutiae was also characteristic of his approach to dogma. Huey was definitely an intellectual who always wanted to be academically, intellectually, and theoretically precise.

When I first met Huey he was living with his secretary Gwen V. Fountaine, whom he later married, in an apartment at 1200 Lakeshore in Oakland. Lakeshore was a high-rise apartment building in a middle-class neighborhood near downtown Oakland that overlooked Lake Merritt. It was nicknamed "The Throne," and it was anything but fancy. Huey and Gwen had moved there in October of 1970 when he was released from prison with the right to a new trial. He had served three years for killing one Oakland policeman and shooting another and by then had made it onto former President Richard Nixon's enemies list.

Gwen was a great partner and made Huey's life easier; she managed a nice home for the two of them and helped with the administrative work of the Party while he worked on the Party's day-to-day business. Huey was refining the ideals in *The Ten-Point Program* and articulating them to the other members, supporters, and recruits. As the leader he exchanged his ideas with them and dealt with the endless legal ramifications that became part and parcel of being a Party leader. Huey was impassioned when he spoke about the Black Panther Party and *The Ten-Point Program*. His physicality, charisma, and intellectual prowess comes through in the iconoclastic photograph of him which remains an enduring image of the Black Panther Party: sitting in a high-backed wicker chair with shields on either side of it, he is wearing the Panther uniform, holding a spear in one hand and a shotgun in the other. This photograph, taken by a photographer described by Bobby Seale in *Seize the Time: The Story of the Black Panther Party and Huey P. Newton* as a "white Mother Country radical," uniquely symbolizes the strength and wrath of a young black man in the 1960s.

Huey loved to challenge me and other young people he mentored by questioning the basic values of our belief systems and having us defend them. He was analytical and well-read and helped me with some of my term papers. He once told me a story about some time he spent in New Haven, Connecticut, where he was working on behalf of Bobby Seale and Ericka Huggins. They were on trial for the murder of Alex Rackley, a 24-year-old Black Panther Party member from New York. At the time there were members of the Black Panther Party who suspected Rackley was a police informant. Bobby and Ericka were subsequently charged with his murder as a means to prevent him from giving up any more information. It was during this trial that Huey first met Erik Erikson, the renowned author and professor of developmental psychology at Harvard University. The two men quickly bonded over the principles of *The Ten-Point Program*, and Erickson saw the validity of their approach.

Huey was not a traditional Christian like me. However, he was a spiritual person who knew the Bible well. He was a philosopher at heart, and I used to sit up all night with him in his apartment, or sometimes I met him at the Lamppost Bar to talk and listen to his theories, just the two of us. We had many things in common like our love of classical music, which we spoke of frequently. Huey had been a serious student of music at a music conservatory and knew how to play the piano. We also had a mutual interest in psychology, which I majored in as an undergraduate.

Huey also helped me out in other ways, like the time he got some of my money back from a con artist who had ripped me off for about $750. I know that he was accused of some bad things and was said to have done drugs and was called a thug, but that's not the person I knew. It's still hard for me to believe all of the things he has been accused of. Although I never saw him do cocaine, he would often retreat to his bedroom and come back sniffling, and he did love his Courvoisier and cigarettes. My friends worried about my safety because I was so close to him and threats followed him everywhere, but he was always respectful and protective of me. When he was living in exile in Cuba because he had jumped bond while awaiting trial for murder, assault, and tax evasion charges, I visited him and Gwen. At the time I was on the staff of Cong. Ron Dellums (D-CA), and was traveling to Cuba on two visits.

While Huey was seen as an intellectual introvert, the Black Panther Party's other leader, Bobby Seale, better known as "the chairman," was the more extroverted of the two. Bobby was smart, charismatic, a brilliant tactician, and a grounded, focused grassroots leader. He is an icon and a hero to me, and I still look up to him. When I first met him, he impressed me as being very nice—a leader always willing to give positive feedback to me and the other "comrades" in the Party. I was known as "Comrade Barbara" at the time. We were and remain close, and I was moved and honored when he attended my college graduation and afterward when he came to my graduation party. My sister Mildred hosted a party at her house, and we spent the night talking and playing cards. Bobby is a good Bid Whist player. For his part, Bobby had dozens of barbeques at different parks and people's homes, and I attended them often because he is a very good cook. He even wrote a cook-book, *Barbeque'n With Bobby Seale*. As a friend, political mentor, and comrade, Bobby always kept an eye on me and kept me safe. I never felt any fear when I was with him. He is a true revolutionary who loves people, and I will always have a special place for him in my heart.

When I first met Elaine, I was intimidated by her but our mutual commitment to the Black Panther Party helped us form a bond that has lasted all these years later. Elaine was commonly misperceived as being a "user," but I was always happy to help her with whatever she needed. We had an honest and straightforward relationship. Like Huey, I shared a love of music with Elaine, and she too was an accomplished musician who sang and played the piano. When I was a staff member on Capitol Hill we worked together on several projects and programs, including one event that was particularly memorable. At the time I worked for Rep. Dellums (D-CA), and Elaine asked me to help her organize a briefing on COINTELPRO (the FBI's Counterintelligence Program) and together we created a successful briefing that even included attendance by political celebrities like Jane Fonda. I have always tried to help her, believed in her skills and talents, and supported her 2005 mayoral campaign in Brunswick, Georgia.

Huey understood the black community needed to have the same self-determination other communities enjoyed. One of his theories was that black people were akin to an oppressed black colony within the United States and that the Black Panthers must organize the socially and politically disenfranchised. The Black Panthers were interested in protecting black people from unjust laws, police brutality, and widespread racism in America, and the group had two strategies for gaining the acceptance and commitment of the "lumpen proletariat." The most notable, and most notorious, was the police patrol. The other strategy, which the Black Panthers considered equally important, although these days it is often over-looked, was the commitment to providing much-needed social services to their communities.

In the decade that included the passage of the Civil Rights Act in 1964, blacks faced more overt racism and violence than is common now, which is inconceivable today, given the history of police brutality toward blacks, particularly in California. To combat the rampant police discrimination that was brought to the nation's attention during the Watts riots in Los Angeles in 1965, a Los Angeles-based group called the Community Alert Patrol (CAP) was formed with a mission to "police the police." Armed only with law books, tape recorders, and walkie-talkies, CAP set out to document and combat illegal police activity. It was Huey who closely followed CAP's progress in the newspapers. Within a couple of months he began to see a pattern of persecution toward members that included them having their equipment destroyed or confiscated before they were beaten, after which they were then arrested and locked up. Such conduct was illegal in Huey's opinion, and he began to study the laws regarding the monitoring of police activity. What he found was that a California Supreme Court decision had stated that "every citizen has a right to stand and observe a police officer carrying out their duty as long as they stand a reasonable distance away."[1] Huey concluded that the actions of the police were a clear violation of CAP's constitutional right to peacefully observe them and state their grievances.

He also noted that the behavior of the Los Angeles Police Department violated the people's First Amendment right to assemble, as well as their Second Amendment right, which says that every man has the right to arm himself. Furthermore, his research discovered that there was a California law that allowed the citizens of the state to carry loaded rifles and shotguns in public. A loaded rifle or shotgun meant an unexpended cartridge in the chamber, and this law also said that unexpended cartridges in the magazine do not constitute a loaded gun. To test the limits of the law, the Black Panthers began to attend rallies and used tactics similar to that of CAP, but added exposed, loaded shotguns. They also began wearing uniforms that consisted of black berets, black slacks, shined black shoes, black gloves, and blue shirts. These police patrols became an integral part of the Party's community policy. Needless to say, although these tactics increased the exposure and membership of the Black Panthers, it did not endear them to the police.

This was particularly true in 1967 when about 30 Black Panthers, mostly armed, went to the California State Assembly in Sacramento to protest a bill introduced by Assemblyman David Donald Mulford that would make it illegal for civilians to carry loaded weapons. The bill passed overwhelmingly so the Black Panthers had to halt the armed patrols but this setback did not deter them. Huey realized that in the eyes of the federal government and law enforcement, if the Party changed direction and moved toward reform programs, they would be perceived as an even more dangerous revolutionary organization.

There is an old collective memory of the Black Panthers as gun-wielding men who wore black berets and dressed in military style clothing and advocated violence. What's wrong with this image is that the good work they did and their efforts to help the poor and other disenfranchised minorities gets lost in the fray and has been forgotten with time. Carrying guns was a way for the Panthers and other blacks to protect themselves and members of their community from the racist tactics police used at that time. The Panthers were earnest about addressing community issues, and they offered people reasonable, immediate aid and gave them practical options for their day-to-day survival. They also provided black people with an opportunity to become empowered in their own right. It was Bobby Seale who stressed the Party's rallying cry "all power to all the people" because he was an advocate of coalition politics. The Black Panthers crossed all racial and ethnic lines during the fast-paced organizing period of the late 1960s. This inclusiveness was a mainstay characteristic of the real power-to-the-people organization that Bobby Seale named the Black Panthers. He was the key national organizer because while Huey was in jail and remained incarcerated during the tragic assassination of Dr. Martin Luther King, Jr., it was Bobby whose leadership helped develop community outreach programs, organized the Party around political issues such as gun reform in California, and institute what was called the U.S. Global Wars of Aggression. Bobby's organizing skills helped the Party quickly spread, growing to more than 5,000 members by opening chapters in Philadelphia, New York, Boston, Chicago, Newark, Omaha, Denver, New Haven, San Diego, and Los Angeles. With 49 chapters around the country, the Party could have a significant sphere of influence, and the membership's diversity brought Party members, community workers, and white leftist radicals together to fight for justice.

When I started working with the party in 1971, it had already begun to become somewhat factionalized between some of the more radicalized militant members and the more mainstream community workers like myself who saw value in their community outreach programs. I worked closely with Elaine Brown, who became the Party's first female chair in 1974, as she focused the Party's work more on the social service aspects of *The Ten-Point Program*. One of my firm commitments to the Black Panthers focused on survival programs, a series that grew to more than 20 social programs providing needed services to black and poor people and promoted an alternative model for problem solving that was based on a more humane social structure. This included much-needed medical programs, such as the first effort to test African Americans for sickle cell anemia; during the first five years of this program more than 1 million people were tested.

The underlying principle of the survival programs was centered on black people becoming organized so that they could survive outside existing governmental systems like Welfare and Medicaid, which were already underserving the black community. Because so many black folks were poor and didn't have food and clothing, the Black Panthers organized "survival rallies," which distributed collections of clothing and food (mostly food), and I enthusiastically helped bag food and distribute it at these rallies.

These rallies had a practical purpose. We used them to conduct voter registration drives and to recruit volunteers and community workers. The Black Panther Party wanted to show the black community that it was relevant and that it could help the people with their daily needs and not just be an ideological political organization. Along the way the Party learned that this was a great way to build support for their organization. It's worth noting that during the time I worked with the survival programs in the early 1970s that various police departments and the FBI engaged in a barrage of tactics meant to discredit or falsely accuse the Black Panthers of crimes and actions that they did not commit. In particular, the Philadelphia and New York offices of the FBI fired off phony letters aimed at discrediting Huey by attacking him and fabricating stories that Party members were stealing food, clothing, and drugs from survival rallies for their own personal use. So much of what the Black Panthers were accused of they were later proven innocent of, or acquitted, but those stories rarely, if ever, were printed in the papers.

As a community member I did a variety of things that involved organizing the community, and in addition to helping the leaders and members directly, I also helped set up the Panther school, the Oakland Community Learning Center. The center was primarily created for the children of Black Panther members and the idea for the school came about one day when Elaine Brown's mother complained to Huey about the poor education her granddaughter could expect to receive when she was old enough to attend school. She was sure that she would not get a good education in the public schools, and she assured Huey that many of the Party's parents and grandparents shared the same view. Huey came up with the concept of a school based on teaching intercommunalism and dialectical materialism, which is characterized by the belief that history is the product of class struggle. He bought and converted a large empty church property that had classrooms and other facilities located in east Oakland on what was then East 14th Street but is now named International Boulevard.

I helped form the corporation, wrote proposals, raised money, and developed the programs. My work was supported by a $500 a month grant from the Youth Project, and this foundation's grants often paid people a stipend to do organizational work in low-income and minority communities. In addition, other kinds of support came in the form of building capacity in local underfunded schools like the Oakland Community School, which in addition to providing kids with an education also fed hungry children as part of the Black Panther Party's Free Breakfast for Children program. When it was first created, this program was castigated by both local and federal government but eventually it was adopted by the national government and became a vital source of food and nutrition to poor children around the country.

It was during this time that I met and closely worked with one of my most vocal detractors, the right-wing writer David Horowitz. At the time he was a strong supporter of the Black Panthers, and he decided he wanted to raise money to buy buildings to house the Panther school. He successfully raised about $100,000, which helped Huey buy the church and some of the surrounding buildings. As Horowitz became more involved with the group he began to play a larger role in operations and served as an unofficial advisor offering advice and resources. He also encouraged the school to hire Betty Van Tanner, his bookkeeper, to handle the books for the school.

In December 1974, Betty and a large sum of money in the Black Panther treasury disappeared and tragically six weeks later, the police found her body. Her head had been bashed in with a blunt instrument and despite the lack of any evidence, Horowitz suspected that Party members had murdered her and stolen the money. This kind of tactic had been seen before and was known to have been used by the government's anti-Panther COINTELPRO group. This prompted Horowitz to leave the organization and from that moment on he waged a campaign of negative statements and never again had anything good to say about anyone associated with the Black Panthers, including me. Despite controversy and misunderstanding, I worked with the Panthers on many projects such as doing key research for Huey's book *Revolutionary Suicide*. Once it was published, I got him $500 from Mills College to have a Black Student Union-sponsored book party and helped get the Panthers involved in voter registration efforts and on Rep. Shirley Chisholm's (D-NY) presidential campaign.

I also ran interference between Huey and Bill Boyette. Boyette was the president of the Cal State Package Store and Tavern Owners Association (Cal-Pack) in 1971 and owned two liquor stores in Oakland. Boyette had asked the Black Panthers to organize a boycott against the Mayfair supermarket chain because they purchased alcoholic beverages from companies that wouldn't employ black truck drivers. The Panthers agreed but stipulated Cal-Pack members would have to make a small weekly donation of money ($10–$20 per store) or goods, as a contribution to the Party's community survival programs. With the Panthers' help, Mayfair was closed in four days and negotiated an agreement with Cal-Pack.

The trouble between Huey and Boyette came when after these terms were agreed to and Boyette was victorious, he proposed a counteroffer of a one-time only donation to the Free Breakfast for School Children program. This would have only provided enough food for one day's serving and when he reneged on his promise to provide weekly donations, the Panthers organized a boycott against his two stores. I advised Huey and Bobby on strategic planning for this boycott but rather than focus on the real issues at hand the national media attention emphasized the fact that the Panthers carried guns. As a result of the media attention there was a significant growth in membership, which in combination with the concern over weapons, drew the attention of COINTELPRO.

COINTELPRO was a covert counterintelligence action program initiated in August 1967 by the FBI. Its mission was to disrupt and neutralize organizations it characterized as "black nationalist hate groups." The Black Panther Party was not initially among these targets, which included the Southern Christian Leadership Conference, the Student Nonviolent Coordinating Committee, the Revolutionary Action Movement, and the Nation of Islam. An FBI memorandum[2] describing the program stated its goals as:

1. Prevention of a coalition of militant Black Nationalist groups;
2. Prevention of the rise of a messiah who could unify and electrify the militant nationalist movement, people like Martin Luther King, Stokely Carmichael, and Elijah Muhammad who the FBI asserted all aspired to this position;
3. Prevention of violence on the part of Black Nationalist groups;
4. Prevention of militant Black Nationalist groups and leaders from gaining respectability by discrediting them; and
5. Prevention of the long-range growth of militant black nationalist organizations, especially among youth.

In September 1968, FBI Director J. Edgar Hoover described the Black Panthers as "the greatest threat to the internal security of the country" and by July 1969, the Black Panthers had become the primary focus of COINTELPRO. Ultimately, it was the target of 233 of the total authorized black nationalist actions. The FBI's counterintelligence program to disrupt and neutralize the Black Panther Party included:[3]

1. The Effort to Promote Violence Between the Black Panther Party and Other Well-Armed, Potentially Violent Organizations;
2. The Effort To Disrupt the Black Panther Party by Promoting Internal Dissension;
3. Covert Efforts To Undermine Support of the Black Panther Party and to Destroy the Party's Public Image;
4. Efforts To Promote Criticism of the Black Panthers in the Mass Media and To Prevent the Black Panther Party and Its Sympathizers from Expressing Their Views; and
5. Cooperation Between the Federal Bureau of Investigation and Local Police Departments in Disrupting the Black Panther Party.

Starting in September 1969, the FBI's headquarters began mobilizing its field offices to share information and work together to attack and crush the Black Panther Party nationwide.

On November 20, 1970, Hoover requested official authorization from Attorney General John Mitchell for "a microphone surveillance and a telephone surveillance at apartment 25A, 1200 Lakeshore, Oakland," which was Huey's residence. Of course, I did not know this at the time, and, as a result, my movements would also be scrutinized by the FBI. They even came to my house to interview me, which of course I refused. I requested my FBI files under the Freedom of Information Act for that period, and when I saw what was on file about me it was hard to believe what I read—and yes, quite scary to see that they had spied on me. It was surreal and I felt violated, as if I had been deluding myself into thinking that I had any real privacy.

In the beginning of February 1971, FBI field offices initiated a flood of anonymous letters to party members, workers, and other people interested in the Party that highlighted information gathered from this illegal surveillance. These letters capitalized on the existence of Huey's alleged "penthouse." In the letters the FBI tried to show that Huey was not only a hypocrite who urged the Party to live simply while he appeared to be indulging in bourgeois comforts, but it made the Panthers look as if their fundraising and other campaigns for the poor were a sham to be exploited for the personal gain of the Party members. This understandably outraged people on both the left and right, and many were duped and taken in by these kinds of stories and shams.

Due to the conflict between COINTELPRO and the Black Panthers, I was placed right in the middle of a movement that, despite its obvious social benefit, was often treacherous and dangerous. I did not then, nor have I ever sanctioned or justified any of the violence associated with the Black Panthers, whether as the result of their own actions or instigated by COINTELPRO agent provocateurs. Prior to the time I started working with the Party, I heard and had read about the virulent behavior that was frequently connected to the Black Panthers, but I could never figure out which shootouts and violent acts associated with the Party were actually caused by them and which ones were committed by COINTELPRO. I gave the Black Panthers the benefit of the doubt because I believed the good the Party did outweighed the bad reputation it sometimes had. I also supported the "Free Huey" movement, which was started in response to his need for legal and financial support after he was jailed for three years on murder and assault charges.

Because of the work I did on the behalf of the Black Panther Party, I too, was under COINTELPRO surveillance and was victimized and smeared by some of its misinformation campaigns. This led some members of the Party to suspect that I was a plant of some kind, and I even received threats. Then, in 1972, when I went to the Democratic Party Convention in Miami as a delegate for Rep. Shirley Chisholm (D-NY) in her campaign for President of the United States, members became even more suspicious of me. There were Black Panthers who accused me of being an FBI agent or simply part of "the system." Although I did not receive any overt threats at the convention, upon my return to Oakland, it was made abundantly clear to me that my presence was not welcome at Party meetings. At one point, I attended a political education meeting and was asked to leave and never come back. I felt that my life had been shattered. How could the people and organization that I had loved and believed in so much and sacrificed so much for do this to me? I was being unfairly persecuted for no reason, could not sleep at night, was very upset, and felt totally lost. I was hurt and intimidated. I told Huey of the situation, and he finally sent word to the rank and file to back off.

On the other side of the spectrum, the "chattering class" of the black bourgeoisie also criticized me but their opinions were not as relevant to me; I believed completely in the values espoused by the Party. When I look back at that time, I suppose I was gullible and impressionable. I fell for some of the Party rhetoric, but I believed in the Party's work to end racism and exploitation. It was the only civil rights group in the Bay Area that made sense to me. For years the Party was at the center of COINTELPRO's hostility toward radical black activism, and the government was able to effectively destroy black political dissent in the United States. This was accomplished by murdering and framing many of the Black Panther Party members, incarcerating its leaders like Bobby Seale, or forcing others, like Huey Newton, into exile. The Party's work became so controversial that even associating with the Black Panthers put anyone at tremendous risk.

Yet for all of the danger and harrowing experiences as a result of my work with the Party, there was a reason God had me walk this road with His guidance. As it says in Ephesians 6:13, "Wherefore take unto you the whole armour of God, that ye may be able to withstand in the evil day, and having done all, to stand."

I am still proud to have played a small role in working with the Black Panthers and often reflect on what a life-transforming experience that was for me. Being a part of the Black Panther movement toughened me up, it made me realize that racism, sexism, economic exploitation, poverty, inequality—all issues we are still dealing with—are a by-product or result of a system of capitalism that relies on cheap labor and keeping people fighting each other rather than uniting and working together for the common good. The haves don't want the have-nots to get ahead and cut into their piece of the pie, and this contributes to the greed, corporate profits, and maintenance of a ruling class that wants to run the world the way it thinks it should be run. In addition, working with the Panthers helped me realize that sometimes working for justice and helping the poor means going against the grain. This is the right thing to do, and I am morally obligated to do what is right. My experience with the Black Panther Party also taught me that while band-aid solutions can be a useful quick fix, we must ensure that all people have their daily survival needs met by changing the laws, policies, and systemic problems that gave rise to the discrimination and economic exploitation.

The reality of our world is that poverty, injustice, racism, and sexism are not an American monopoly, and in response the Panthers were also an international organization. Through my work with the Party, I learned how domestic policy issues are interconnected on an international level and how what we do here can have global repercussions. Contrary to conventional wisdom, the Panthers were not a black nationalist organization and did not preach hatred toward white folks. Although the Party recognized the beauty and power of being a person of African descent, this did not exclude having white friends or working with people of any race, as long as those relationships were based on mutual respect and concern for the human family. The Panthers had a lot of white supporters, and Huey and Bobby convinced me that my anger and frustration must not be toward white people as a group, but rather the economic system and system of government that fosters racism, hatred, and division.

In many ways, this militant, revolutionary organization mellowed me out. The late David Dubois, the stepson of W.E.B. Dubois, one of the founders of the NAACP, worked as the editor of the Black Panther Party Newspaper. We became friends and his probing intellect and gentle spirit was like a solid rock for me during that transformative period. The principles as outlined in *The Ten-Point Program* were consistent with the eight Beatitudes in the Bible, so they were consistent with my religious and moral values. The Panthers helped me become more loving toward everyone and took away some of my bitterness. They helped me become more understanding and tolerant about people I deplored and helped me recognize that white people could be victims of America's sins just as much as blacks or other groups like Native Americans, Latinos, and Asian Pacific Islanders. In *Soul On Ice*, Eldridge Cleaver writes that, "it's essential to relate the mind to the body where the government becomes the mind that leads the people and gives them proper representation." I am very proud to be part of the "mind of the government" and to be trusted by my constituents to represent them.

Huey and Bobby had a falling out around 1975 or 1976 and by then, I was living in Washington, DC, working for Rep. Dellums (D-CA). It was around this time that I came across a newspaper article that reported Bobby had left the Party, and my heart just sank. I was totally blown away. No matter where Bobby and many of the other members of the Party have gone, I have tried to keep friendships alive. I still stay in touch with Bobby and Elaine, and I'm pleased that I stayed in contact with Huey until his death in 1989. In 2004, I was deeply honored to officiate at the wedding of Huey's stepson, Kieron Slaughter to Alice Thompson.

Notes

1. David Hilliard, *Huey: Spirit of the Panther* (Thunder Mouth Press, 2006), p. 43.

2. *The FBI'S Covert Action Program to Destroy the Black Panther Party. Book III: Supplementary Detailed Staff Reports on Intelligence Activities and the Rights of Americans*, p. 187. See http://www.aarclibrary.org/publib/church/reports/book3/html/ChurchB3_0097a.htm.

3. *FBI's Covert Action Program*, pp. 189–223.

❦

Chapter Four

The life of the nation is secure only while the nation is honest, truthful, and virtuous.

—Frederick Douglass

Let me begin by saying that I recognize that the world is a dangerous place and that terrorism is real. And we must do everything to prevent another terrorist attack and ensure that our country is safe and prepared. As a member of Congress who took the oath of office to "support and defend the Constitution of the United States against all enemies, foreign and domestic," I have and will remain true to this oath. However, I do not believe the Bush administration has effectively implemented the recommendations made by the 9/11 Commission that would make America safer, nor do I believe that the policy of preemptive military strikes will reduce tensions and eliminate terrorism. Although complex and difficult, there are smart and effective strategies that will achieve our national security goals and reshape America's role and image in the world. March 19, 2008 marked the fifth anniversary of the illegal, immoral, and strategically foolhardy invasion of Iraq. Five years into our occupation of this now-devastated nation, it is important to reflect on what got us into the Iraq quagmire—namely the Bush administration's simplistic view of world affairs and its overly militaristic foreign policy, and of course, as many believe, oil. It's instructive for my fellow members of Congress and the American people to look back to that fateful day on September 14, 2001, if we are to understand how Congress enabled the administration to pursue war-making policies that have reduced our country's security and tarnished our reputation as a global peacemaker and defender of human rights.

It was important that the President and the Congress address the anguish of people whose loved ones had died in the attacks and whose bodies still had not been recovered. I agonized over the suffering of the victims, the volunteers, fire, police, and rescue workers, as well as the grief of the friends, families, and co-workers left behind. Members of Congress were sincere in their concern for the victims and their families in their response, but revenge and retaliation motivated many of their actions.

Then, Congress voted almost unanimously to give President Bush a "blank check" to attack an unspecified country, an unspecified enemy for an unspecified period of time and all those who harbored the terrorists after the horrific 9/11 attacks in New York and Washington, DC and hijacked the fourth plane, Flt. 93, which ultimately crashed into a field near Shanksville, Pennsylvania. I stood alone against this "blank check" for what has become known as the Global War on Terror. I knew then that the administration would turn it into a Global War and tried to warn the nation and my colleagues in the Congress. Since then, I have organized aggressively in the Congress—and across the nation—to prevent Bush's doctrine of pre-emptive war. I voted against Bush's senseless war in Iraq, and I am working to prevent him from launching another war against Iran. Despite the fierce criticism levied against me then, I am proud to have stood alone on the right side of history that day, on the right side of the law, and on the right side of what would have been best for United States security for both the short and long term. Similarly condemned by many in government in the 1960s, the Rev. Dr. Martin Luther King, Jr. stood on the right side of history when he audaciously spoke out against the Vietnam War and urged African Americans to end their silence about the horrible tragedy and policy of the Vietnam War. His position inspired me in 2001 and continues to inspire me throughout my career in public service. African Americans have a responsibility to speak out against the Bush administration's zealot strategy of "go it alone" and "take military action against countries at will." We must speak out because the President and his minions have made the world less, not more safe, and they have compromised the security of every American. I am using all of my capacity—as first vice-Chair of the Congressional Black Caucus (CBC), as co-Chair of the Congressional Progressive Caucus, as a co-founder of the Out-of-Iraq Caucus, and as a member of the House Appropriations Committee and Foreign Affairs Committee—to end this foolishness and return our nation to a moral and strategically sound course. As a social worker, mother, grandmother, and daughter of a career military officer, I know that our country must organize against these irresponsible policies and exploits if we are to confront the deep pain and suffering that is everywhere in our community. Dr. King saw this. He knew that the "bombs we were dropping in Vietnam were exploding in the ghettos of America." It is no less true today when we have spent over $500 billion on this war and occupation and know from estimates that we could ultimately spend $3 trillion dollars to fight a war that should never have been started but can't find the moral or political will to spend money on our own people living in poverty and abject hopelessness. It's not just a moral issue about war, although it is surely that. It is a moral issue about priorities, about what our nation believes in and holds dear, about what our future holds. As I write this chapter, I must pause and pay tribute to two phenomenal women, Cong. Maxine Waters (D-CA) and Cong. Lynn Woolsey (D-CA). They have worked tirelessly to end this occupation of Iraq and are brilliant legislators, and I am proud to be part of what was called, coined by Cong. Woolsey: "the triad." Cong. Waters founded the Out-of-Iraq Caucus with me and Cong. Woolsey as co-founders, and we will not rest until all of our young men, women, and contractors are out of Iraq. And the future is about the survival of the generations to come.

I will continue to stand steadfast at the forefront of Congressional efforts to put a stop to this so-called "Global War on Terror" and all that it has done to devastate our nation. We must start with the war in Iraq. This is not hindsight or the changed view of one who now looks at the carnage and says, "Oops, I made a mistake." We fought against it then. In the Congressional debates that started well before the invasion of Iraq, I along with a number of my CBC and Progressive Caucus colleagues argued against a pre-emptive strike against Iraq and stated our concerns about its ensuing consequences—all of which have unfolded over the last five years. During the debate on the resolution that authorized the president to use military force against Iraq in October 2002, I offered a substitute that would have allowed United Nations and international experts to continue inspections for weapons of mass destruction. Unfortunately, only 72 members out of the 435-member House of Representatives voted for this substitute. The world now knows what many of us then believed: there were no weapons of mass destruction in Iraq. At the same time, the world now knows what's been confirmed: that there was no operational relationship between Saddam Hussein and al-Qaeda.

Consider how things would have been different had we not invaded and occupied Iraq. We could have sustained the sanctions that prevented Saddam Hussein from reacquiring weapons of mass destruction. We would not so dramatically have destabilized the Middle East region, inviting Iran into Iraq to play a more dominant role. Our military would not be stretched thin and, of course, 4,000 men and women in uniform would not be dead, and tens of thousands others would not have been seriously injured. We would not have killed approximately 100,000 Iraqis, and we would not have earned the enmity of the "Arab Street" and the scorn of nations around the world—many of them allies and friends—for our willful violation of international law. And, Congress would be able to dedicate much-needed resources here at home for domestic priorities. For these reasons, my colleagues in the Out-of-Iraq Caucus and I have opposed providing the president with a continuing "blank check" for waging war and occupation in Iraq. Instead, we propose funding for protecting the troops on the ground and bringing them back home safely. This is what we call "fully funded redeployment."

And the American public is way ahead of Congress about this issue. In fall 2007, 70 percent of those surveyed rejected giving the president further funding for Iraq without condition; and people favored requiring funds be spent on redeployment over providing the administration funds without conditions by a two-to-one margin. Twenty-four percent of Americans supported voting against the funding, and nearly half supported providing funding only for redeployment. Bolstered by such overwhelming support from the American people, I have been working to build support in Congress for fully funding redeployment and cutting funding for occupation and combat operations. In July 2007, 94 members joined Reps. Lynn Woolsey (D-CA) and Maxine Waters (D-CA) and me in sending a letter to the president that said that the only funding we would vote for was to protect the troops and contractors and bring them home.

Let me be clear—all of our troops and contractors should come home. That's why I have worked with my colleagues to include a provision to prohibit permanent military bases in Iraq. We were successful in including this language in a number of authorizing and appropriations bills as well as a stand-alone bill, which passed the House in July 2007 by an overwhelming bipartisan vote. Yet, despite the fact that the president signed these provisions into law five times since 2006, he issued a statement as he signed the fiscal year 2008 Department of Defense (DOD) authorization bill into law, that showed he intended to ignore the provision that banned permanent military bases—which was part of the administration's unconstitutional assertion of a presidential power, a blatant violation of the law and the constitutional oath of office that he had twice taken "to see that the laws are faithfully executed." I was extremely disappointed, yet not surprised.

Bush's administration continued to take the Nixonian view that the president was above the law. President Bush gave every indication that the United States intended to be a permanent presence in Iraq. This was borne out by the use of DOD and administration euphemisms such as "enduring bases" or "contingency operating bases" rather than "permanent," given that the previous terms were less likely to raise the ire of the Iraqi people or the suspicions of Americans. Was it really a coincidence that members of the cabinet, the administration, and the *Declaration of Principles for a Long-Term Relationship of Cooperation and Friendship Between the Republic of Iraq and the United States of America* issued by the White House on November 26, 2007, repeatedly used the word "enduring" each time they referenced the U.S. presence in Iraq? A closer look revealed a blueprint for how the two countries planned to set the foundation for the future of America's involvement in Iraq.

Sadly, the White House's pattern of behavior seemed to indicate that they were intent on cutting Congress out of any decisions related to the permanent stationing of the U.S. military in Iraq. Without formal Congressional input, President Bush and Prime Minister Nouri al-Malaki set the stage for future agreements on the disposition of U.S. troops in Iraq. What was so dangerous about the

language of the *Declaration of Principles* was that it included a provision where the U.S. promised to preserve the Iraqi government's
stability and protect it from "internal and external threats," and
thus increased the likelihood that any agreement like this one
would be considered a treaty by legal experts. However, under the
Constitution, the president cannot unilaterally enter into treaties;
this prerogative rests with Congress. Kenneth Katzman, a Middle
East analyst at the Congressional Research Service, stated then
that, "The *Declaration of Principles* would appear to commit the
United States to keeping the elected Iraqi government in power
against internal threats," and "I leave it to the lawyers to determine
whether that's the definition of a treaty or not but it certainly seems
to be—is going to be—a hefty U.S. commitment to Iraq for a long
time."[1] If this commitment is honored by the United States it
would be unprecedented in the history of American foreign policy.
The administration's vehement denials that the provisions of preserving Iraq's stability from "internal and external threats" didn't
make the *Declarations of Principles* a treaty was its way of hiding the
fact that the *Declarations of Principles*, like H.J. Res. 64, was an attempt to create an imperial presidency. During two hearings I questioned Secretary of State Condoleezza Rice and Deputy Secretary
of State John Negroponte on whether they believed our policy was
to build permanent military bases in Iraq, and they both unequivo-
cally said no. I told Negroponte that he should inform the president
of this.

The White House made it clear that it had no intention of discussing this with Congress and, instead, administration officials argued that the president had the authority to broker a "status-of-
forces" agreement without Congressional approval. The United
States has roughly 100 "status-of-forces" agreements or military relationships with many countries around the world including Germany, Japan, and South Korea. In mid-December 2007, Raed Jarrar, an Iraqi political activist, pointed out that, "Bases of the U.S.

around the world are not situated in an occupied country. For example, U.S. forces in Japan can't just go out of their bases and [set up] a checkpoint in Tokyo. They can't go around Tokyo arresting Japanese people."[2] What was more to the point in this instance was that there was no agreement in place anywhere in the world, where the United States guaranteed to preserve and maintain the stability of a country's government. In addition, in countries where we have "status-of-forces" agreements, the U.S. military is prohibited from getting involved in internal security as has been seen by our lack of pledge of military involvement during two coups that overthrew governments in South Korea.

To make certain that the Bush *Declaration Of Principles* did not end up being a backdoor attempt to keep our troops in Iraq indefinitely— or as Sen. John McCain (R-AZ) said, "for 100 years," I introduced a bill that required that any formal agreement that emerged from the *Declaration of Principles* must have first obtained Congressional approval. Further, my bill stated a sense of Congress that the Iraqi Parliament should put its imprimatur on any agreement as well. Finally, this measure prohibited funding for any agreement that may have emerged from these "principles" that did not have the approval of the House and Senate. On May 22, 2008, the House passed my amendment to the Defense Authorization Bill by a bipartisan vote of 234 to 183 to require Congressional authorization before committing the U.S. military to such a long term presence.

At the same time as we have been working to end the occupation of Iraq and ensure that we don't have permanent military bases there, my colleagues and I have been leading the charge in Congress to ensure that we do not launch another pre-emptive war— this time against Iran. Like many of my colleagues in December 2007, I was surprised to learn that our nation's 16 intelligence agencies concluded in their National Intelligence Estimate (NIE) that not only had Iran halted its covert nuclear weapons program in 2003, but that this program remains frozen. The NIE noted that the leaders in Iran had responded to world opinion in stopping the program, suggesting that diplomacy was a more powerful strategy than the threat of the use of force. As promising as this development was, it didn't mean that the United States could let down its guard. Rather, we should engage in aggressive diplomacy with the support of the International Atomic Energy Agency and our allies to ensure that Iran does not become a nuclear weapons proliferator. Our greatest danger was that the president's and vice president's continued saber rattling would derail such efforts, and as was the case with the invasion in Iraq, potentially set back the cause of United States security for a generation.

That's why I worked with my colleagues to ensure that such posturing did not turn into a march to war with Iran. This was also precisely the reason Congress must demand that the administration pursue a path of diplomacy in seeking to deflect Iran from acting upon any nuclear weapons aspirations it may harbor. To prevent a pre-emptive strike against Iran and urge the administration to redouble its diplomatic efforts, I introduced two bills. The first, the Iran Nuclear Accountability Act, prohibited the use of U.S. taxpayer funds to carry out any covert action to force regime change in Iran or carry out any military action against Iran in the absence of an imminent threat to the United States. The second, the Iran Diplomatic Accountability Act, posited that one of the important first steps in dealing with Iran must be to ensure that we have direct, comprehensive, and unconditional bilateral talks between our two nations. To facilitate this goal, my bill required the administration to show it was serious in this endeavor by appointing a high-level official or special envoy to Iran and ensure that this envoy received the necessary support to carry out this diplomatic mission. Initiatives like these were developed to deter the administration from plunging us into another war of choice. Because the administration did not take the military option off the table, I continued to persist in my efforts to see that Congress removed it.

As precarious as conditions in Iraq and Iran were, however, I want to take a moment to put them into context and point out how they were part of an even more dangerous pattern. Simply put, I saw the war in Iraq and posturing with Iran as but two in a series of examples that demonstrated the Bush administration's dedication to a unilateral, militaristic foreign policy. Instead of focusing on diplomacy and nonproliferation efforts, instead of collaborating with allies in both diplomatic and military fields, the Bush administration was intent on pushing belligerent pre-emption. This strained our alliances, stretched our troops to the breaking point, and bankrupted our treasury. All the while the administration's policies actually encouraged and facilitated nuclear proliferation.

Let me give you three examples.

The first is the United States–India nuclear deal that the administration and the Republican Congress forced through in 2006. This deal, which was put on hold because of Indian coalition politics, would have effectively gutted nearly four decades of nonproliferation regime. By abandoning our allegiance to the Nuclear Non-Proliferation Treaty (NPT), we opened the door to other nations doing the same thing. Our blatant refusal to adhere to the NPT made our condemnation of North Korea's nuclear programs smack of hypocrisy and rang hollow in many capitals around the world.

Second, consider the administration's continued funding of weapons systems for a threat that no longer existed. Dr. Larry Korb, former Assistant Secretary of Defense under President Ronald Reagan, now with the Center for American Progress, proposed that by simply eliminating a portion of the Defense Department's budget that had been funding Cold War-era weapons systems, we could have recouped $60 billion and reinvested it into our communities. Rep. Lynn Woolsey (D-CA) and I introduced this idea as legislation called the Common Sense Budget Act. We needed to move past our own reliance on these weapons of mass destruction if we were to create a world in which we could successfully build pressure to prevent others from acquiring them.

Finally, take the example of the Bush administration's sale of weapons and weapons technologies to Saudi Arabia and some of its neighbors in the region. Some estimate that when all told the sale reached upwards of $20 billion. Given the region's history and the fundamental reality that you cannot buy peace through arms, in what world did it make sense to ignite an arms race in this tinderbox of a region? That's why I joined with my colleagues Reps. Anthony Weiner (D-NY) and Robert Wexler (D-FL) and introduced legislation to block the latest slice of this sale to Saudi Arabia. These examples provide compelling reasons to heed Dr. King's prophetic call to speak out so our voices can be heard, as he did 40 years ago. He cautioned that, "A nation that continues year after year to spend more money on military defense than on programs of social uplift is approaching spiritual death."[3] That statement is as true today as it was then. And it is just as true today that the folly of our military adventurism and misplaced priorities is exploding in our cities every day.

Today as we explore the state of black America, the Native American, Latino, Asian, Pacific Islander communities, and the plight of the poor, we must examine the economic conditions of our communities. Americans must not be silent about the dramatic and negative impact that the reckless military escapades of the Bush administration have had on African Americans and other minorities—and indeed on all Americans. We cannot separate the two—they are as inextricably linked today as they were forty years ago while Dr. King was leading his moral crusade against the war in Vietnam. I urge you to demand that the United States reorder its national priorities, that we follow a principled and effective foreign policy that is rooted in the respect for law and the effective use of multilateral and bilateral diplomacy; that we eschew war and violence as the means of "getting our way" in the world; and that we respect cultural, religious, and political differences, and we insist on democratic principles and the respect for internationally recognized human rights. Leadership is needed in this fundamental struggle. Let us continue to redeem the prophetic legacy of Dr. King and give honor to the meaning of his struggle and sacrifice by moving this nation onto the path of peace and reconciliation. This is my prayer each and every day.

Notes

1. Steve Inskeep and Guy Raz, "U.S., Iraq Ponder Long-Term Treaty," National Public Radio's Morning Edition, January 24, 2008. <http://www.npr.org/templates/story/story.php?storyId=18368586.>

2. Inskeep and Raz.

3. Martin Luther King, Jr. (James Melvin Washington, ed.), A Testament of Hope: The Essential Writing and Speeches of Martin Luther King, Jr. (Harper: San Francisco, 1986), p. 241.

✂

Chapter Five

I have crossed over on the backs of Sojourner Truth, Harriet
Tubman, Fannie Lou Hamer, and Madam C. J. Walker. Because of them I can now live the dream. I am the seed of the
free, and I know it. I intend to bear great fruit.

—Oprah Winfrey

As a "sister," I view the world through a different lens, and my
prism has been faceted by discrimination from two angles—as an
African American and as a woman. Fighting against both of these
prejudices has been yet another obstacle in my journey, but each
experience, failure, and success, like those experienced by my
mother, have only made me stronger and more determined to clear
the twin hurdles of race and gender. When I was a child living in
El Paso, I was blessed with strong female role models—my mother
and my teachers, the Sisters of Loretto. My mother was, and is, a
wonderful, self-assured woman, and the Sisters of Loretto taught
me that women can be strong, independent, spiritual, and set an
example for others by living by their convictions. Under their tute-
lage I learned the Old Testament story of Queen Esther, whose
bravery inspires me and to whom I turn to as a role model.[1]

Just as with Esther, there have been times in my life and in our country's history that, I too, have been called on to stand up, be counted, and speak for those who cannot. Throughout our history, there have been people who have stood by and said nothing—as when the Native Americans were killed in a genocidal race to steal their land, the effects of which have never been atoned for or remedied. From our founding fathers to plantation owners and farmers, in the early days of our country, great men and women spoke of the freedom and liberty of people yet owned slaves and stood by and allowed the evils of slavery to continue only to be replaced by segregation. Despite the brief period of freedom and civil rights that was afforded former slaves after the Civil War, Reconstruction came to an abrupt end in 1877. Then in 1883, the Supreme Court dealt free blacks and their quest for equal rights yet another blow when it consolidated five different segregation cases[2] into one case, *The Civil Rights Cases* (1883),[3] with one overriding issue—that the Civil Rights Act passed by Congress in 1875, which was written to protect blacks from private acts of discrimination, was unconstitutional. The Supreme Court's decision was handed down by a vote of 7–1. The majority opinion, written by Justice Joseph P. Bradley, declared that the Civil Rights Act of 1875 was unconstitutional. It held that the equal protection clause of the fourteenth Amendment applied only to state action and not privately owned businesses, essentially creating a federally sanctioned system of segregation that allowed each state to determine for itself how to treat blacks. Despite the outcome of the Civil War and the passage of a major piece of civil rights legislation, the Supreme Court upheld the constitutionality of racial segregation, even in public places, under the doctrine of "separate but equal." Bradley wrote that it was time for blacks to assume "the rank of a mere citizen" and stop being the "special favorite of the laws," which coincidentally was the same argument used to eliminate affirmative action programs in both public and private matters.

In the sole dissenting opinion, Justice John Marshall Harlan wrote that "hotels, amusement parks, and public conveyances were public services that operated under state permission and thus were subject to public control." It was not long after the court's decision that southern states began enacting sweeping segregation legislation which became known as Jim Crow Laws. These laws not only prohibited blacks from sharing public spaces with whites, they also helped to disenfranchise blacks and led to brutal acts of mob violence, lynchings, and other forms of terrorism from groups like the KKK. It's estimated that from 1889 to 1930, more than 3,700 men and women were lynched in the United States, mostly in the South.

Despite the overwhelming and widespread abuses and human rights violations being heaped on blacks in America, there were brave people who continued to fight injustice who clung tenaciously to the tenets of the Constitution and the Bill of Rights. One important example of this came in 1890. In that year Louisiana passed Act 111, which specifically required "separate but equal" accommodations for blacks and whites on railroads, including separate railway cars. A group of black and white citizens from New Orleans were undeterred by this flagrant violation of the civil rights of all blacks and decided to test the constitutionality of Act 111 by having a light-skinned African American named Homère Plessy board a train car reserved for whites. He, of course, was quickly arrested and a local judge, John H. Ferguson, ruled against Plessy. Later in *Plessy v. Ferguson* (1896), the U.S. Supreme Court upheld Judge Ferguson's ruling and asserted that Plessy's rights were not denied because the separate accommodations provided to blacks were equal to those provided to whites.[4] Justice Henry Billings Brown, who wrote the majority opinion, stated that "separate but equal" accommodations did not stamp the "colored race with a badge of inferiority." In one of the great legal dissents in American history, Justice Harlan wrote, "Our Constitution is color-blind, and neither

knows nor tolerates classes among citizens," and as a result generations of free black Americans were subjected to vile treatment and
accommodations that were generally inferior to those provided to
white Americans, even though federal law specifically prohibited
this. State and local laws required that public schools and places
and transportation like trains and buses have separate facilities for
whites and blacks and as a consequence "separate but equal" remained standard doctrine in U.S. law until its final repudiation in
the later Supreme Court decision *Brown v. Board of Education of
Topeka, Kansas* (1954) and its companion case, *Bolling v. Sharpe*
(1954).

When I was growing up, the reality was that black citizens did
not have the same access to services white citizens did. As we realize now, "separate but equal" really meant "separate and unequal."
Like millions of other black Americans, my wonderful family raised
me to live my life with dignity, but in the face of daily humiliation
and discrimination it was always difficult for me to hold my head
high when everywhere I looked I was told that blacks were inferior
to whites. I saw it in "colored-only" drinking fountains. I was denied admittance to movie theaters in El Paso, although we could go
to the movies at Fort Bliss. My family, including my stepfather, Bill
Massey who was an army officer who had served his country
proudly, were turned away at a drive-in restaurant in Hueco, Texas.
And, of course, there was the issue of segregated public schools. It
seemed like I was always living in two different worlds: I went to a
Catholic school with Latinos and caucasians, but then went home
to a neighborhood that was mostly black and Latino, a duality that
made me feel self-conscious, as if I was never a citizen of the America reserved solely for whites. About the time I reached elementary
school age, some of the parents of children at Fort Bliss began to officially protest segregation and in an October 1952 *El Paso Herald-
Post* article, one protest was noted. In a letter written by Clarence

Mitchell, director of the Washington Bureau of the NAACP, to Secretary of Defense Robert A. Lovett, Mitchell asserted that black children could not attend the schools at Fort Bliss and had to be bused to Douglass, one of only four schools in El Paso at the time which educated black students, which was also where my mother and aunts had attended school. Douglass provided an exemplary education for black students, and like my mother and aunts, graduates of Douglass were smart, well-prepared, and very successful as adults.

However, white parents were allowed to send their children to school on the army post. This letter also noted that segregation in schools had been abolished on military posts in other states. It was not until May of 1954 when the U.S. Supreme Court ruled in *Brown v. Board of Education*, that racially segregated public schools violated the Constitution. Schools were required to show good faith compliance with this ruling at the earliest practical date. For El Paso, it was September 1955 when for the first time, black students had a choice of attending Douglass, Bowie, Jefferson, or Austin schools during the 1955–1956 school year. I was in the third grade. Concerned about uprooting me from my friends and teachers at St. Joseph's, which had always been an integrated school, my parents felt that I should stay at St. Joseph's. Although I loved school, I had to walk a tight rope between my white, Catholic friends at St. Joseph's, and the other black and Latino children who lived in my neighborhood, who attended different schools. I felt displaced and often it seemed like I did not have a place to be me.

History class was particularly difficult. I didn't know any more about black history than any other child did back then, and Africa seemed a far-off land that you only read about in books. Like most students my age, I thought Africa was a country, not a continent and at that time black or African History was not even taught as a subject. My only frame of reference for my people's history in Africa and here in America came from white people whose views on blacks ranged from outright bigotry to paternalistic condescension. And when World History was covered in class it was the traditional white, Western European curriculum that was taught, a narrow ethnocentric view of history to say the least. As I learned my history lessons, I couldn't quite put my finger on it, but I knew something was terribly wrong with this version of history. It wasn't until I was in my 20s that I completely understood that my ancestors had been brought here in chains and forced to work as slaves to build this country. I also had not made the connection between the mistreatment of black Americans, Jim Crow, and segregation and how all of these systematic ways of discriminating against blacks were related to the institution of slavery. At some level, I think I was in denial about this, given what little I knew about slavery. Being black made me feel ashamed, bad, and insecure because "slaves were slaves."

Years later, still feeling scarred by this experience, I wrote a letter to my music teacher at St. Joseph's who was an Irish American woman named Julia Buchanan. Her words in response were a great comfort to me, and I keep them in my Bible to this day. She said in part:

> The human race is endowed with a spine, and among its other duties, it is to keep the head erect. I want you to quit wilting. You said that the girls at school used to look at you when the word "negro" was mentioned. So what? When I first went to El Paso, as a little kid of eight, the girls generally made fun of my physical appearance, my clothes, my hair, and looks. Even then, I had a fighting heart, and sized them up as being vulgar and ill-bred. Children are sometimes cruel because they have not been properly trained at home. You and I were properly trained by our mothers, we were lucky. When you first came to school, I paid no more attention to the color of your skin than to any other child. You were a shy little girl, and I soon

learned that you were the brightest one in the class. That is why I loved you.

When we moved to the West Coast, I quickly learned that life for African Americans in California in the 1960s wasn't much better than it was in Texas. Segregation was as institutionalized there as it had been in El Paso. I saw poverty, a lack of jobs, and drug abuse in neighborhoods large and small filled with primarily blacks and Latinos, and I began to understand institutional racism as it was manifest in the ghettos and barrios of Southern California. Housing segregation existed in California until the Byron Rumford Fair Housing Act of 1964, and although schools weren't segregated, housing patterns fostered de facto segregation. That's why busing to achieve racial integration was a big issue in California. In fact, de facto segregation hit me head-on when I decided I wanted to be a cheerleader at San Fernando High School in California. No black girl had ever been a cheerleader there, and I was determined to change the selection rules so that the entire student body could vote on the selection process rather than a small committee of white folks. I knew that I was as good as anyone else, so I went to other black students and said, "Look, these rules are wrong. They're keeping us all from being cheerleaders."

At the time, I was participating in a work-study program and worked four hours a day at the Pacoima Memorial Lutheran Credit Union. My starting wage was $1.00 an hour, although I eventually got a raise to $1.25 an hour. My first boss, John Mance, was a member of the board of the NAACP, and when I told him about my high school dilemma, he helped me get the NAACP involved in my cause. Carl McCraven, the CEO of the credit union was also the Chairman of the Board of the local division of the NAACP. I told them what was going on at school regarding the rules for cheerleading tryouts and with their help and that of the NAACP we were able to get the school to change the process of electing cheerleaders. We created a democratic process that gave me or any-one at the school the chance to try out in front of the whole school rather than as part of a clique. When the selection was made, I was elected and became the first black cheerleader in the school's his-tory. I may have had to shake things up to do this, but I paved the way for many young African American girls to cheer our teams to victory at San Fernando High School, "YEA Tigers."

Today, *Brown v. Board of Education* is still the law of the land, but it is no longer a national reality. The legal walls of segregation have been replaced in many areas by de facto segregation in our neigh-borhoods and communities and each year our schools are becoming less and less integrated, and in too many cases, integration has van-ished from some schools. In California there is one more weapon in the arsenal of segregation that has been used to great detriment and that is Proposition 209, which unfortunately was pushed by an African American man, Ward Connerly with the help of former Gov. Pete Wilson. Proposition 209 effectively ended affirmative ac-tion in public institutions of higher education, contracting, and employment in California, and it has repeatedly shut out African Americans from full participation in state employment and con-tracting at the University of California system.

It's hard to believe that in 1964, I graduated from high school, was a young bride of seventeen married to a young man in the mil-itary and then moved thousands of miles across the United States and the Atlantic Ocean to live in Upper Heyford, England. This was quite a change from my life in America, and I moved there to join my husband Carl who was stationed at a military base in Eng-land. We were perfectly located for traveling throughout the coun-try and on the continent. Our time together in England was fun, lively, and entertaining. Europe was a fascinating place, and I was introduced to new cultures and languages and gained a new per-spective of the world around me. While we lived in England, we bought a toy poodle we named Cognac, and I drove our little Fiat all over Europe for two summers. Living on a different continent gave me more exposure to other people of African and Caribbean descent, and I soon realized that although I was a daughter of America, I was also a daughter of Africa. Unlike in the United States where I was led to believe I was a racial minority, I realized my roots to Africa made me a part of something much bigger. All of a sudden it hit me like a rock—I was part of the majority of the world's population which is over two-thirds people of color. This was an empowering and liberating revelation. Not knowing how and when I would do it, I became determined that I needed to share this insight with other black people at home and vowed that one day I would make a pilgrimage to the Caribbean and Africa to see for myself what it finally felt like to be in the majority.

And what better time to do this than in the 1960s, which is when I reached maturity. It took the birth of my two sons, divorce, and going to college as a single mother to help me become more independent, but the 1960s were a time of radical change, and I matured as a woman and a person during that era. This was before the passage of the Civil Rights Act of 1964, and it was an era of enlightenment and actualization for women and minorities. Being a politically active young adult at the end of the 1960s had a profound effect on me. After starting college at Mills in the early 1970s, I began reading about black and African history and took classes in sociology and ethics. One day, my ethics professor required us to answer the question, "Was slavery wrong?" By now, I felt like I finally understood the forces at work that led to the slavery of Africans and how those forces changed the history of African Americans and led to segregation and further injustice. I felt confident that I could answer the question for myself and help explain to others the damage and negative impact that centuries of slavery and then segregation had had on the lives and personal identities of

black people and how it continued to destroy the self-esteem and feelings of self-worth of black children everywhere. I concluded in my paper that the institution of slavery was wrong because it dehumanized
human beings—both the slave owner and the slave. I was beginning
to understand more about the source of my low self-esteem and why I
sometimes felt insecure around white folks. This process of reading
and learning made me come to grips with why some black people
acted like so-called Uncle Toms. The dehumanization of people is a
heavy burden to bear, and it leaves emotional and psychological scars
that are passed down from parent to child for generations. I had not
escaped this legacy any more than any other black American.

I was filled with outrage at what slavery had done to my psyche
and countless other black people for centuries, and I turned my
anger onto my government and aimed it at a country that had illegally brought my ancestors to America against their will and bound
them in chains in the cargo holds of the dreaded slave ships that
were often a death sentence during passage. Slavery may have come
to an end but the suffering and long-term effects of its horrors on
the spirit of black people had not. No matter how brave as soldiers,
how intelligent, well educated, or talented as artists, blacks were
not regarded as equal to whites. The indignities endured by a large
segment of our population were either ignored by whites who
turned a blind eye, left unchallenged by people who felt helpless
about how to bring about an end to the suffering of blacks, or they
were perpetrated by bigots and hate mongers on a large scale day in
and day out.

Both my father and stepfather had served and protected our country in the army for 25 years and at least two wars. How could they,
and hundreds of thousands of other black soldiers, be expected to go
to foreign countries to fight for other people's freedom only to return
home to an America where racism, segregation, and degradation
were legally institutionalized by the government? As African Americans we carry a deep pain in our hearts about our exploitation as a

people. African Americans played an equal and essential role in building and defending our country. If we are to chart a peaceful and productive path and move forward as a unified country that is not divided along racial lines, we must come to grips with the realities of this dark past and deal with the ramifications for African Americans and its effect on our history. Even though I was only in my early twenties at the time, the realization of how much slavery influenced my people and what a corroding injustice it was, was an epiphany for me. It was the first time I understood at a visceral and intellectual level, the long-term psychological, economic, social, and dehumanizing effects of racism and its roots on generations of blacks. I could not accept this as the status quo any longer, and I knew that combating this injustice was why I was put on this earth.

It was around this time that God proved to me that I was on the right path because that was when Rep. Shirley Chisholm (D-NY) first came into my life. Through her example and her gift of friendship and faith in me, she became someone I could look up to as a role model, not just as an adult figure, but as an African American woman and first African American and first woman to seriously run for the presidency of the United States of America, Shirley was the first African American woman elected to Congress, and when she visited Mills College, she had just recently announced she was running for President of the United States. I was shocked at the time because even though I was president of the Black Student Union and had invited her to speak at my school, I didn't know anything about her announcement. The media had not considered her run newsworthy enough to broadcast, and I just couldn't believe that they had neglected to report on the first African American woman running for the presidency of the United States of America. Her campaign slogan was, "I am unbought and unbossed and a catalyst for change!" and from the minute I heard the slogan I knew I wanted to achieve an unbossed, unbought life too and that I wanted to help others do the same.

Shirley Chisholm's eloquent speech at Mills College centered around the power of women and people of color to change the world and told us why different perspectives should be a part of the policymaking process. I was so inspired by her call to action that I got up the nerve to approach her. I told her I was taking a course taught by Dr. Fran Mullins that required me to get involved in a presidential campaign. But I was conflicted in my heart and didn't feel I could work for the leading Democratic contenders: Sens. Edmund Muskie (ME), George McGovern (SD), and Hubert Humphrey (MN). I was starting to accept the fact I would probably flunk the class as a result. I also told her that I was inspired by her platform and the example she set for other black women, and I let her know that that I wanted to volunteer to work for her campaign. This was the first time I had ever met a politician who I truly felt was working to give me a voice because she understood the experiences I had had and could relate to my concerns.

Once she said to me, "If you really want to shake things up and change the system, you must get involved in politics. So stop telling me you don't believe politics isn't relevant." Then she asked me if I was registered to vote, and when I said no she really took me to task about that! She explained that her campaign was being organized and run from the ground up and said, "We don't have a lot of national money, so if you believe in me you'll have to get it started yourself." I took this challenge and helped organize her Northern California presidential campaign right out of my government class at Mills and became a campaign coordinator. Joining me were Wilson Riles, Jr., Sandré Swanson, who eventually became my Congressional Chief of Staff and is now a member of the California State Legislature, Sandy Gaines, then the student body president, Huey Newton, and Bobby Seale. I made sure I was registered to vote for her in the primary, and we developed and organized a coalition of people of color and worked to get white women involved too. It was a struggle getting the whole coalition to pull together behind a black woman, but we did it—and took about 10 percent of the Alameda County vote in the process. Through our hard work, some of us were elected as delegates to the 1972 National Democratic Convention in Miami, that is until the chair of the California delegation, Assemblyman, later to become speaker and mayor of San Francisco, Willie Brown made his famous "give me back my delegation" speech and won the battle for California to be a "winner take all" state. We may have been stripped of our delegate status but we found a way to remain on the floor for the entire week and participated in all of the meetings and caucuses at the convention. And I ended up getting an A in a class that I had been prepared to flunk.

After working on her election, Shirley Chisholm became my mentor and taught me to understand how important it is to mentor women, whether it's providing an internship, staff position, helping them work within community organizations, giving them recommendations, or helping them get military commissions and find jobs. A former teacher in the Bedford-Stuyvesant section of Brooklyn, New York, Shirley Chisholm spoke fluent Spanish and was a true Renaissance woman. "Mrs. C," as we called her, was a great advocate for education and immigrant rights. She worked to address poverty and was an early opponent of the Vietnam War. She recognized that economic justice and equal opportunity for all is central to the struggle for justice and human rights. "Mrs. C" always regarded me as the little girl with the big Afro with two small boys in tow who sought her attention and counsel. Impeccably dressed, she always sported high heels, even after her eyesight began to decline. At one point when I ran for the California legislature in the early 1990s she even offered to give me some of her "business-like attire," which, unfortunately, was too small.

"Mrs. C" exuded fun and joy during her lifetime. She was the same age as my mother and loved to dance. One year, at my mother's birthday party, she and Shirley danced the night away with men young and old. They "hung out" on the dance floor longer and with more energy than us younger folks. People were always inspired by their contact with Shirley, and she definitely helped me gain support for my candidacy when I ran for the state assembly. When she noticed that my schedule was too hectic, a state of affairs that hasn't changed one bit even today, she counseled that I needed quiet time for reflection. "You need to stop in the middle of the day, quietly eat lunch, and regroup." I try to remember to heed her advice but it's so hard to slow down everyday given the hectic pace of congressional life and work.

At my victory ball celebration that was held after I had won the state senate race in 1996, "Mrs. C" announced at that event that she knew one day I would become a member of Congress. The statement caught me completely off guard, and after I overcame my initial shock, I asked her what she meant. She replied in her usual stern tone, "I can see things that others don't."

To honor her lifelong fight for justice, in 2001, I introduced a resolution in the House of Representatives that was passed by a vote of 415–0. When the now famous HR 97—a resolution celebrating her life and accomplishments—was being debated from the House floor, I called from the floor to tell her to watch it on C-Span. She was concerned because there were so few Republicans speaking out on behalf of the resolution, and she was worried that the tradition of bipartisan spirit was not what it had been when she was in Congress. The inclusiveness of the past had been replaced with polarization and divisiveness. Shirley emphasized that when she had been in Congress, she had Republican friends and had worked across party lines to get the job done. Although she was really excited about this resolution, she was also disappointed that more Republicans weren't giving it their support. Well, I really felt her pain and said, "don't worry, Republicans do remember you and your work and do support the resolution." Instead of letting it pass on a voice vote, which typically happens when a resolution is on the suspension calendar and noncontroversial, I called for a roll call vote. To my delight every Democrat and Republican and one Independent voted yes. When I called her back after the recorded vote she was very happy and relieved. This resolution recognized the enduring contributions, heroic achievements, and dedicated work of the first African American woman elected to the U.S. House of Representatives, Shirley Chisholm. The resolution said in part:

> Ms. Chisholm's mission to include women, children, African Americans, and other minorities in public policy opened the door to a whole new debate lacking in Congress during that time. She is a remarkable woman who paved the way for many of us by fighting throughout her life for fundamental human rights. Ms. Chisholm has devoted her life to public service. She has been a committed advocate for progressive causes, including improving education, ending discrimination, increasing the availability of child care and expanding the coverage of the Federal minimum wage laws to include domestic employment.

She passed away in January 2005, and I attended her funeral in Palm Coast, Florida. I was overcome with sadness, and I took her death very hard. I know that if she were still with us, she would implore us to stand up against the injustice that created the poverty in our country which Hurricane Katrina revealed for the world to see. She would challenge us to work to eliminate it. She'd ask, "What are you doing sitting around? Why aren't you working to eradicate poverty, homelessness, and hunger?" She would also insist we fight to have our civil liberties and civil rights upheld and that we participate in our political system so we can fight against the neglect which is leading us to, as in Queen Esther's time, the destruction of our people. She would say, "It's time to get out of Iraq" and tell us to oppose this war as vigorously as we can. That's what she would say. Congresswoman Shirley Chisholm definitely went against the grain and was a true radical. I have been fortunate in my life to have met women of great stature who have fiercely fought for what they believed in, risked life and limb to speak out against terrible injustice, and have sacrificed personal comfort and safety to lead others down the path of righteousness.

One woman in particular has been a guiding beacon of light in our time and has shown what true courage and fearlessness means. This woman was an American woman of the twentieth century who was also a role model of mine, Coretta Scott King. With her dignity, compassion, intellect, and moral authority, Mrs. King's life also embodies the story of Esther. There is no doubt in my mind that Mrs. King was born for a time such as hers. She joined her husband on the front lines of the civil rights movement and made it her life's work to ensure that the fight for civil rights and the non-violent struggle for justice and peace continued. It is well known that Mrs. King and her family faced daily threats of personal peril during the 1950s and 1960s. Not only was her husband arrested for civil disobedience, but he was also beaten and stabbed. Their home was bombed, and their phone rang with hate calls at all hours of the day and night. I had a short-lived experience with this form of harassment when I voted against giving President Bush a "blank check" to wage pre-emptive war in perpetuity, and I don't know how she managed to endure this harrowing situation for so long.

Like Huey Newton, Coretta Scott King was a victim of warrantless domestic surveillance by the FBI. Despite the very real threats against her family and the assassination of her husband and others who fought for justice, Mrs. King stood tall at each crossroad of injustice. She was not afraid to confront injustice whenever she saw it, she stood for what was morally and ethically right, and she knew that peace must transcend race, gender, sexual orientation, age, disabilities and national boundaries. Coretta displayed great leadership in the fight to end apartheid in South Africa. She clearly opposed our immoral occupation of Iraq, and she was determined to fight against homophobia. On November 22, 2002, she was in California to accept the Circles of Hope Award for her work opposing discrimination against the gay community and during the acceptance speech she made this eloquent statement that bridged the gap between America's intolerance of minorities both at home and abroad.

> We need more proactive education against bigotry and intolerance in America's schools, so young people are not seduced by the poisonous propaganda of hate groups. Most importantly of all, if we want to create a more nonviolent society, we should be very concerned about our country getting involved in a war. A war with Iraq will increase anti-American sentiment, create more terrorists and drain as much as 200 billion taxpayer dollars (as of 2008, going on 500 billion) which should be invested in human development here in America.[5]

In the next part of her speech, she stated her support for me and said:

> And here I want to take a moment to congratulate Representative Barbara Lee for her courageous stand as the only member of Congress to vote against waging war in the Mideast. I'm very proud of you, Representative Lee, and I think your constituents are much blessed to have the benefit of your leadership.

After the horrific events of 9/11, she publicly stood with me when I found myself the only member of Congress who voted "no" in giving the Bush administration a "blank check" to go to war. She didn't have to do that, but she did. She counseled me stating, "You must remember Martin's quest for peace through nonviolence as part of your work as a member of Congress." This was quite a challenge. But I am going to continue to speak out against the occupation of Iraq and against the irresponsible policy of pre-emptive war no matter how personally difficult it might be. This pre-emptive policy doesn't make any sense, does nothing to strengthen our national security, and it's wrong. Coretta confirmed that for me.

Betty Shabazz was another woman who like Esther understood the need to step forward and set an example to her people. As a single mother, she was yet another role model for me, a tower of strength, and a woman whose life demonstrated what it means to be a leader. She was in nursing school when she met Malcolm X, and after they were married she received her bachelor of science degree in nursing from the Brooklyn State Hospital School of Nursing. After his death, she was left to raise six girls by herself, and Dr. Shabazz was determined to set an example for her daughters and show them that they could be smart, accomplished, and strive for excellence. She did so by continuing her own education despite overwhelming odds and earned a bachelor of arts in public health education from Jersey City State College, a master of arts in public health education from Jersey City State College, and a PhD in education administration from the University of Massachusetts at Amherst.

Although plagued with many personal disasters, she kept her focus on racial, social, and economic justice. Our country will miss Dr. Shabazz as we attempt to enter into an honest dialogue on race relations. As the loving widow of El-Hajj Malik El-Shabazz (Malcolm X), Betty carried the torch for racial and religious reconciliation throughout the world. Her spirit is so strong and so alive I am convinced that her painful departure from this earth will provide the impetus for people, especially children, to learn more about her and Malcolm X. When I first contemplated running for public office in 1989, Betty Shabazz and another woman of courage, Maudelle Shirek, the former vice-Mayor of Berkeley who is now in her late 1990s and taught me so much, sat me down to discuss my candidacy. In Betty's warm, loving, yet tough manner, she told me to stay on track and not let cynics and doubters deter my efforts. She reminded me of all of the obstacles that I'd face as an African American woman in public office, but she also told me that the inner strengths that I relied on that had helped me to successfully raise two children, would help me tackle this new challenge. In remembering Dr. Betty Shabazz, I must thank God that my life has been blessed by her counsel and guidance.

There are so many other strong African American women who have been leaders that history has ignored and who we don't pay tribute to nearly enough these days. Women like Phillis Wheatley, who was sold into slavery as a child but later, as an adult had her book of poetry published, making it the first book of its kind to be published in America by a former slave. With the passage of time, women of all races have joined her ranks and their contributions, even when left unnoticed or unheralded, have left indelible marks on our nation's history. But it is African American women like Harriet Tubman, the unfaltering and fearless conductor of the Underground Railroad; Sojourner Truth, the proudly determined former slave who was a leader of the abolitionist movement; Judge Constance Baker Motley, the ninth child in a family of 12 that immigrated here from the West Indies who was a recognized jurist and legal scholar and represented James H. Meredith in 1962 in his fight to attend the then all-white University of Mississippi and was the first African American woman to sit on a federal bench in 1966; and the first African American woman elected to the United States Congress, my dear friend and mentor, Rep. Shirley Chisholm (D-NY), who took office in 1968.

I am proud to be the 171st Woman, the 100th African American, and the 19th African American woman to receive the privilege of serving as a member of Congress. It was not that long ago—1916 in fact—that a Montana social worker named Jeannette Rankin became the first female member of Congress, the first woman elected to the U.S. House of Representatives, and to date the only woman to be elected to Congress from Montana. She was a lifelong pacifist, advocated for peace, women's rights, women's suffrage, and she staunchly voted against America's entry into the world wars; notably she was the only member of Congress to oppose the declaration of war on Japan. And she, too, was a social worker.

Although not an elected member of Congress and often described as a mild-mannered seamstress, there is one woman in particular who has had an enormous impact on our nation's history, and that woman was Rosa Parks. By many accounts, Rosa Parks was an ordinary woman, yet she possessed a quiet strength and nobility and worked hard her entire life, all the while suffering the daily humiliation of segregation and discrimination. It doesn't take much to imagine Rosa Parks being bone tired and just wanting to sit down after a long hard day of work only to be subjected to the indignity of being forced to ride in the back of the bus. She is famous for her refusal on December 1, 1955, to obey bus driver James Blake's demand that she relinquish her seat to a white man. Her subsequent arrest and trial for this act of civil disobedience triggered the Montgomery Bus Boycott, one of the largest and most successful mass movements against racial segregation in our history. This simple act of nonviolent defiance also propelled Martin Luther King, Jr., one of the organizers of the boycott, to the forefront of the civil rights movement. Rosa Parks changed the course of American history. She represented all oppressed people that day and became the symbolic mother of the modern civil rights movement. In June of 1999, she received the Congressional Gold Medal of Honor and in 2005, I cosponsored a bill introduced by our beloved, late great Congresswoman Julia Carson of Indiana, which President Bush signed into law. The bill authorized the carving of a statue of Mrs. Parks to be placed in the United States Capitol Rotunda. She is the first African American woman to receive this honor. When Mother Parks sat down that day in 1955, she stood up to be counted. She did not set out to topple Jim Crow, she was simply a dignified woman of color who was emotionally, physically, and morally exhausted by the inherently unfair way she had been treated her entire life. She took it upon herself to make a brave gesture and in so doing compelled others to join her to try to put an end to an injustice, and for this we owe her an enormous debt of gratitude. When she took her stand by simply sitting, Rosa Parks bucked the norm. She went against the tide and put America closer to realizing the right of "liberty and justice for all." She knew what a perilous risk it was, just as Dr. King and his wife recognized the risks they were taking. But Rosa also knew if she did not take a stand at that moment—and on that bus, the lynchings, beatings, and bombings would continue and it would mean, as in the time of Queen Esther, the inevitable destruction of her people.

Another woman who stood head and shoulders above her peers was my beloved friend and colleague, the late Patsy Mink, who in 1965 became the first woman of color, the first Asian American, and the first woman from Hawaii elected to Congress. She introduced the groundbreaking Title IX legislation, which requires federally funded colleges to provide women with equal education and athletic opportunities. She graciously extended her hospitality to my mother, sisters, and me on our vacation in Hawaii, and she was a true champion of the underrepresented. And now for the first time, we have a magnificent woman, and one of California's greatest representatives, who is serving as the first woman Speaker of the House—Nancy Pelosi. Both Patsy and Nancy had to swim upstream but just look at what they did as they too went against the tide.

Women of all races, religions, and ethnic groups face the same obstacles, and we all have glass ceilings, but if we follow the example of the brave women who came before us and those who are with us now, it is possible to break through that ceiling. It will not be easy, but we have to stand up for what we believe in and fight for what is right, despite what others might do to keep us down and defeat us. On one occasion in 1999, I, along with a group of other Congresswomen led by Rep. Lynn Woolsey (D-CA), were ordered removed from a Senate hearing by Jesse Helms (R-NC). Our crime? We had the audacity to disrupt the meeting by trying to present him with a letter supporting an international treaty against sexual discrimination that was signed by more than 100 House members urging a vote on the treaty. This treaty had been signed by President Jimmy Carter in 1980 and was ratified by 162 countries. But since taking over as Chairman of the House Foreign Relations Committee four years earlier, Helms had successfully blocked the treaty. After asking us to "please act like ladies," Helms directed Capitol Police to escort us from the hearing room. This was just one more example of the complete lack of serious attention that is paid to the issue of women's rights as an integral part of the fight for human rights.

Like other members of the Congressional Black Caucus (CBC), I work on a daily basis to eliminate the disparities that exist between minorities and majorities. I believe if you don't respond accordingly, you can't change the system and the conditions which have given rise to racism, sexism, and tragic economic disparities that result in poverty and lead to the spread of diseases such as HIV/AIDS. The CBC is playing an active role in leading this country in the public policy debate on these issues, and I think that we are the conscience of the Congress. CBC members work day and night for these causes and are committed to economic development, justice, fairness, and freedom, not only for black communities but for all Americans.

Notes

1. The story of Esther comes to us from the Book of Esther in the Old Testament when many Jews from the kingdom of Egypt had been captured and enslaved by the Persians. Esther was a Jewish woman who had been orphaned as a child and was raised by her uncle Mordecai, who had been a slave but was elevated to the position of court advisor to the Persian King Ahasuerus, more commonly known as Xerxes the Great, son of Darius. The story of Esther is an example of the sentiment "God works in mysterious ways" and is often cited as such in both the Jewish and Christian faiths because Esther bravely stood and was counted when her people needed her help the most. Esther was a stunning beauty and the king, seeking a new wife, was holding a beauty pageant at the court so that he could choose the most beautiful woman in the kingdom for his next wife. It was then that Mordecai encouraged Esther to enter the contest knowing that she would be chosen. But he warned her that she must never reveal that she was Jewish. Overcome by her beauty King Ahasuerus chose her as the winner of the beauty contest and wanted to make her his wife. She married him and became his queen, all the time keeping her Jewish identity a secret. Little did she know though that God had plans for her and the Jewish people. The court of King Ahasuerus was a dangerous place to live, and it was filled with intrigue and betrayal; the king was constantly on guard against plots to kill him and take over the throne and the kingdom. Surrounded as he was by traitors and provocateurs, it didn't take long for two of his ministers, Bigthan and Teresh, to show their true colors. They had a plan to kill the king. Mordecai learned of their plot, told Queen Esther about it, and she then reported it to the king. The king, upon learning of the treachery, ordered that the two ministers be hanged. King Ahasuerus then chose a man named Haman as his senior minister, and this man demanded complete loyalty of everyone in the king's service. He ordered all to bow down to him but Mordecai refused, saying that as a Jew he was forbidden to bow down to a man; he explained that Jews bowed down only to God. This enraged Haman and to get his revenge he decreed that not only would Mordecai be hanged, but he ordered the massacre of all of the Jews in Persia. To execute Mordecai,

Haman ordered the construction of a very tall gallows and to determine the day for carrying out the execution of the Jews, Haman cast lots, or "purim." Once the day was chosen, the news spread throughout the kingdom and Mordecai, realizing that it would mean the end of all the Jews, knew that his people's only hope for salvation lay with Esther. He convinced her that she must reveal her true identity to the king, tell him of Haman's plans, and plead for her people. Initially, Esther was afraid and knew that she could not ask this of the king because no one spoke to the king unless summoned, to which Mordecai responded with this famous passage from the Book of Esther in chapter 4, verses 12:14: "Do not think that because you are in the king's house you alone of all the Jews will escape. For if you remain silent at this time, relief and deliverance for the Jews will arise from another place, but you and your father's family will perish. And who knows but that you have come to royal position for such a time as this?"

Esther summoned up the courage and at a large feast, revealed her identity to the king, and told him of Haman's plot to massacre the Jews and hang her uncle. The king agreed to save her people and on the same day that the Jews were to be slaughtered, the king ordered Haman to be hung from his own gallows; in thanks and celebration for their deliverance, the Jews now observe this day as the holiday called Purim.

2. The individual cases were *United States v. Stanley, United States v. Ryan, United States v. Nichols, United States v. Singleton,* and *Robinson et. ux. v. Memphis & Charleston R.R. Co.*

3. *The Civil Rights Cases,* 109 U.S. 3 (1883).

4. *Plessy v. Ferguson,* 163 U.S. 537 (1896).

5. Coretta Scott King, "Address by Coretta Scott King," Circles of Hope Dinner, San Francisco, California, November 22, 2002. See www.margieadam.com/action/csking.htm.

Chapter Six

> We want to be in control of our lives. . . . And when the government erodes that control, we are not comfortable.
>
> —Barbara Jordan

This has been the hardest chapter for me to write. It's very personal, yet I am convinced that I must tell this part of my story to help parents, teachers, politicians, and young people understand that there are millions of other women who have somehow "made it" who have been through many of the same traumas of youth and young adulthood that I did. I hope I am able to convey the absolute necessity for honesty when informing young girls and boys about their sexuality and the methods of contraception available to them. This honesty and objectiveness is needed to help policymakers make the correct decision in support of comprehensive sex education programs and in preserving a woman's right to choose, which is upheld in *Roe v. Wade*; when it comes to issues of procreation, sexuality, and family planning, I believe strongly that government should stay out of the private lives of individuals. If I can accomplish this, then the anxiety and pain I experienced while writing this chapter were worth it.

Confusion, loneliness, uncertainty, exhilaration, angst, pain, and ambivalence—teenagers feel all of these emotions and then some, and I certainly wasn't any different. Raging hormones, peer pressure, and the stress of school life makes for one heck of a roller coaster ride when you're a teenager. Once we're adults we tend to develop a form of emotional amnesia: although we can vividly recall embarrassing or painful experiences, we forget that one of the reasons this phase of life is so difficult is that the problem-solving part of the brain isn't fully developed, which is the only explanation I can come up with to explain some of my own mistakes. By the time I was 13, I was a boy-crazed girl going through intense physical and emotional changes but when it came to sexuality and relationships I was completely in the dark. I hadn't the foggiest idea about how my body functioned or how you got pregnant. Although I was attracted to boys, I didn't know how their bodies worked either so I was constantly worried about getting pregnant from things that had nothing to do with procreation.

I daydreamed constantly about boys at school, but especially about certain boys like David, Bubba, Roger, and George. I went on a few dates with these boys, but most of my contact with them was just in passing on the street or at school, or I imagined romantic scenes with them in my daydreams. I would devise silly schoolgirl plots in my head so that I could "just happen" to run into them or maybe get a chance to talk to them, especially Bubba, who lived just two houses away from me. I would sit for hours on the front porch of Papa's house, hoping that he would walk by so I could find a reason to get him to stop and talk to me.

David was another boy who lived in my neighborhood, and we both liked each other and did everything we could to spend time together, but my grandfather was strict and he wasn't having any of that. Even if David came to the front door and asked if he could visit with me, my grandfather forbade me from seeing David. This of course only made me that much more determined to see him, and I became bold and defiant of Papa's wishes. I could be just as stubborn as he was when I wanted something, and I wanted a boyfriend more than anything. Because David couldn't come to see me, I figured I would go to him and that's how I began sneaking out of the house and going to parties. I wanted to be with him no matter what. He was exactly the kind of boy that teenage girls fall for and get crushes on. He was tall, about six feet two or so, and very nice. David tried to cultivate a "bad boy" image by smoking and acting cool but he was just a nice young boy.

At the time, I was an avid reader of *True Story* magazine, and a lot of what I learned about relationships and sex came from between the covers of the magazine, which was the worst possible place to learn about anything, let alone boys and sex. This was the 1950s and there just weren't any books that we could read that would give us accurate and honest information. And sex education in Catholic school was unthinkable. As an adolescent, being around boys was confusing. Most of the time I didn't really understand why my body reacted to contact with boys in such weird and unpredictable ways. It felt like the physical and emotional parts of my life were an ever-changing drama of awkward, perplexing, and undecipherable inter-actions with boys that left me feeling unsure about my body and my-self. I was completely lost when it came to how to deal with boys. Sometimes when I slow danced with David, I could feel his body re-acting to our bodies being pressed up against each other, and I knew that something was happening to him, but I wasn't sure what it was or what it meant. There were times after we danced a slow dance to-gether that I would become terrified; was convinced that somehow this kind of contact could lead to my becoming pregnant. After-wards, I would pray for days and then check my stomach to see if it was getting larger, or if I was putting on weight.

My ignorance of sex and how you got pregnant made me wary of everything and put me in a perpetual state of anxiety, and I was scared about something all the time. My family was also preparing to move to California, which just added to my stress and anxiety and made me a nervous wreck. I was petrified of the move and couldn't bear the thought of leaving behind El Paso and everything and everyone I had known growing up. The familiarity of my school, friends, neighborhood, and church was a source of comfort to me. Having these comforting and familiar parts of my life yanked out from underneath me left me feeling adrift. In my schoolgirl mind, the idea of saying goodbye to David and Bubba was like a tragic love story I had read in *True Story*, and it filled me with sadness and longing. But as I wrote in my diary, which I did for at least ten years, the night we left for our car trip to Southern California, I was determined to make something out of my life so I could rectify some of the terrible humiliations black people had endured, including my family and me. On that hot June day in El Paso in 1960, I began a road trip with my mother, stepfather, and sisters that started an unimaginable life's journey. I had no idea at the time, but the move to California would monumentally change me in ways that forever altered me as a person and changed the course of my life. By the time I was a junior in high school, I had built up the courage to become an advocate of black civil rights and was instrumental in getting the local chapter of the NAACP to help me change my school's racist cheerleader selection policies. I had gotten pregnant and got married to my child's father Carl and then had a miscarriage, all the while continuing to be married, but in secret. Carl went off to college but lived with his parents, and I went back to high school as if nothing had ever happened. Unfortunately, Carl and I let our hormones do our thinking for us, and we nervously continued to have sex, in spite of the risk it involved. We were pretty clueless about how one quick decision to have sex could be so significant, considering what birth control options were in those days, and I of course got pregnant again.

Barbara Lee at San Fernando High School, San Fernando, California, where she was the first African American cheerleader, 1963.

Mayor and former Congressman Ron Dellums at his fundraiser in 1984.

Barbara Lee at work on Capitol Hill, 1976–77. (Courtesy of the author)

Barbara Lee in Otuam, central Ghana, at enstoolment as Queen Mother Nana Araba Mboraba II, December 14, 1994.

Barbara Lee in Darfur, Sudan, 2005.

From left to right: Craig Lee, Shirley Chisholm, Barbara Lee, Auntie Juanita (Franklin), Auntie Lois (Murrell), and Uncle Melvyn (Murrell), Oakland, California, 1990. (Courtesy of Cleo's Photography, Oakland, California)

Children, grandchildren, and daughters-in-law (left to right): Angela Lee, Tony Lee, Barbara Lee, Jordan Lee, Simone Lee, Craig Lee, Memuna Lee, Jonah Lee, and Joshua Lee, Oakland, California, 2007

Barbara Lee with President Bill Clinton at a fundraiser in San Francisco, California, 2006.

Meeting with the late Secretary of Commerce Ron Brown and legislators at the state capitol, Sacramento, California, 1994.

Barbara Lee with Congresswoman Shirley Chisholm in Detroit, Michigan, in 1989 at the National Political Congress of Black Women.

Barbara Lee with Gloria Steinem at the March for Women's Lives in Washington, D.C., April 25, 2004. (Courtesy of the author)

Barbara and Mildred Tutt, Girl Scout Troop 151, El Paso, Texas, circa 1956.

Papa (W.C. Parish), Beverly Hardy (Tutt), Mildred Whitfield (Tutt), and Barbara Lee, El Paso, Texas, 1958

Sisters (from left to right): Barbara Lee, Mildred Whitfield, Beverly Hardy, Mother's Day, 1957. (Courtesy of the author)

Three-year-old Barbara in 1949. (Courtesy of the author)

Wedding, Bill and Barbara, 1969.

Barbara Lee, Beverly Hardy, Mildred Massey, Mildred Whitfield, Hawaii, 2003. (Courtesy of the author)

Marisol Ashwell, Kristen Scott-Maklary, Barbara Lee, and Rev. Cecil Williams, at the twentieth anniversary of the March on Washington in 1983. (Courtesy of the author)

Barbara Lee receiving Honorary Doctorate at Mills College in 1999.

Mills College commencement speaker Barbara Lee with President Janet Holmgren, 1999.

Left to right, Beverly Hardy, Mildred Whitfield, Auntie Juanita, and Barbara Lee at Auntie Juanita's 96th birthday party in 2007. (Courtesy of the author)

Mills College graduation, 1973 (left to right): Stepfather William Massey, mother Mildred Massey, Barbara Lee, and sons Craig Lee and Tony Lee. (Courtesy of the author)

Barbara Lee, junior prom, San Fernando High School, San Fernando, California, 1963. (Courtesy of the author)

This was years before the sexual revolution and although the birth control pill had already been discovered, it certainly was not widely available, and the most common forms of birth control in the early 1960s were abstinence, infrequent sex, the withdrawal method, spermicidal douching, condoms, diaphragms, and the rhythm method and taking quinine pills, and sitting in a hot tub of water if you thought you might be pregnant. Needless to say, we all know how reliable these forms of birth control have been. Just take one look at birth rates. When these methods failed, which they usually did, women who didn't want to have a baby were left with little or no safe and legal options for ending an unwanted or unintended pregnancy. They could try to get an abortion in one of the states where abortion was legal, but in many states, that was only allowed if it could be proven that the abortion was needed to protect the health of the mother. Most other women had to go either underground and search for back alley abortions or go overseas. Finding myself pregnant again and still in high school was like some kind of horrible nightmare that I kept hoping I would wake up from. Carl and I had never sat down and seriously made plans for our future together because we lived such separate lives, and I went to school as a married woman with none of my classmates the wiser. Carl was away in the Air Force, and in the course of things, we had never really considered what having a baby would mean to our lives together, or our futures.

As if my getting pregnant wasn't enough complication for two teenagers to handle, Carl then got deployed to England on a military assignment. There I was facing a second pregnancy with my husband being shipped overseas, and I had no idea why my life had spiraled out of control. The turmoil was hard to bear, and this time things were different because I didn't have a miscarriage but I was faced with the same terrible dilemma. What was I going to do about having a baby? There was no way I was going to have an abortion and back then there were no networks that provided any kind of social services to pregnant teens. Teen pregnancy was certainly not publicly flaunted or socially accepted and sexual attitudes in the early 1960s dictated that pregnant young women were expected to keep silent about their situation and hide it from everyone. I had to find an answer, and quickly. I could go to one of the many homes for unwed mothers that were out of town, and like the other young girls there, I could have my baby in secret too. In these homes for unwed mothers, girls were expected to give their babies up for adoption once the child was born. They were then expected to return home after their absence as if nothing had ever happened. The girl's family often offered explanations like she had been recuperating from a prolonged illness, or she had been visiting a sick relative out of town.

This was such a moral and social conundrum. Here I was married but unable to have my child because we had kept our marriage a secret and the stigma of what would be perceived as an unwed pregnancy was too horrible to imagine. And if I dropped out of school to have the baby, I not only couldn't keep it, but I could pretty much count on not going to college or having any future. The more I thought about my situation, the more I kept coming back to the same solution: I had to get an abortion. As morally reprehensible as I felt it was, this decision could also have terrifying physical ramifications. Not every state allowed safe legal abortions, and illegal septic abortions were a primary killer of African American women in the 1960s; this was more than a decade before a woman's right to choose became federal law. At the time, any abortion performed in a state where abortion was illegal was called "back alley," and although many of these illegal abortions were provided by doctors and midwives with the best of intentions who worked with little or no money in less than optimum circumstances, there wasn't any guarantee that you wouldn't end up with the other kind of abortion—one performed by anyone of hundreds of evil heartless people who were out there posing as doctors who performed abortions in conditions that were filthy and little more than butcheries that endangered the life of the woman.

These quacks weren't caregivers concerned about the health and welfare of women; they just took their money and committed horrific crimes on women's bodies, often leaving them to die slow painful deaths. In many cases, they showed little if any concern whether a woman lived or died, got sick or infected, or if a botched abortion would damage a woman's reproductive organs so badly, she would never be able to have children.[1]

Knowing how dangerous abortion was and at a loss for what to decide, I told my mother about my predicament and she sent me to El Paso to get help from a friend of hers who was a Latina. She was one of my mother's best friends and a former coworker. If not for her, I wouldn't have had any idea how to get a safe abortion. She had all sorts of connections in Mexico since El Paso was on one side of the Rio Grande River which acted as the border between Texas and Mexico. She helped arrange for my abortion and then took me across to Juarez, Mexico. Unlike most black women whose only options were to have the child or risk a slow, horrible end from infection or bleeding to death, I didn't have to go to a butchery where the procedures were performed in a back alley by some quack. On the other hand, given a choice, I wouldn't have had any medical procedure performed in the quasi-clinic where my abortion was performed. But in the 1960s, we did what we had to do. The place seemed relatively clean and safe, and a short Mexican doctor with a white coat handled everything. Most of the unbearably painful procedure and aftermath are a blur, and I was so young and scared that I blocked most of the day from my memory and only vaguely remember being in the operating room. Thankfully, it wasn't a long or difficult trip home, and my mother's friend brought me back to El Paso after the procedure.

The anguish, guilt, and sorrow that I felt about having an abortion is painful to think about even today. But as hard as it was to make, I knew that this decision would change my life forever, and that for me, it was the only way I could finish high school and be able to go on to college, which luckily I was able to do. After graduating from Mills College in 1973 with a degree in psychology, I decided I wanted to attend graduate school to pursue a degree in clinical psychology to address many of the societal ills that affect poor black women and how those stresses break them down as human beings. In my application to Berkeley, from which I received my MSW, I wrote:

> I would like to plan my curriculum very carefully so that I will have a strong clinical background but in conjunction with various social institutions and politicians that I see a therapist must work closely with. My professional ambitions are not to get the PhD in order to get a high paying job. What I hope this degree will provide is the necessary tool for me to open a Free Mental Health Clinic where psychologists, psychiatrists and social workers would have a new framework to work within. I visualize this clinic as one which is interconnected with all institutions, agencies and political organizations which contribute to the misery of the patients. Therapy would be a very important part of this clinic but social programs, research, and actual concrete solutions to various problems would be an integral part. I would like to begin designing such a comprehensive clinic as part of my graduate work.

I was admitted into a PhD program in psychology at the California School for Professional Psychology but decided to attend the master's degree program in social welfare because I had received a HUD fellowship to continue my education and it could only be used for a master's program. I enrolled in the community mental health track, which had an emphasis on clinical work and psychotherapy. I believe social services must not only help with band-aid solutions like short-term emergency or immediate direct assistance, but they must also work to change policies that contribute to depression, psychosis, etc. To that end, psychiatric social workers must help empower people in distress to take control of their lives and take on the institutions that are part of the problem. For example, if a woman can't afford day care and she becomes angry and impatient with her kids, the therapist's job is to help her develop coping mechanisms so she can learn to deal with her frustration before taking her anger out on her children. If she can handle stress better, then we can empower her to seek redress for the lack of day care. Developing skills that will help her tackle local government can show her how to find a way to address the shortage of affordable, reliable, and safe day care. A good therapist helps people take charge of their destiny, and that kind of empowerment and activism requires political and community action.

While I was still in graduate school and taking a course in community mental health, I was able to reach the goals outlined in my graduate school application by founding the Community Health Alliance for Neighborhood Growth and Education (CHANGE, Inc.). One of the community mental health course requirements was to identify a problem in local community mental health services, analyze the solutions that were being implemented, and propose an alternative. As part of the community mental health program at Berkeley, all candidates for a master's in social welfare were required to do a clinical internship. I did mine at two different places, the Highland Hospital inpatient psychiatric ward and the Berkeley outpatient psychiatric clinic. Right away I noticed that both facilities lacked treatment approaches and therapies that were relevant to African Americans, and I used my identification of this problem as the subject of my paper. I decided that instead of making my practical clinical experience simply an academic one, I would turn my term paper into a proposal and try to set up my own mental health clinic that had a focus on the African American community and the issues that they dealt with on a daily basis. I used the final paper, my research, data theory, and other elements as the basis for the proposal to start CHANGE.

The first point of my plan was that mental health services had to be demystified so people would feel comfortable coming to a clinic to seek its services, which was why I named the organization CHANGE. Secondly, the treatment needed to have an emphasis on psychotherapy because depression among poor African Americans is high. Advocacy, prevention, and education were important for this model of treatment because people are worn down by the day-in and day-out stresses of not having enough money to pay rent, feed a family, get medical treatment, pay for child care, find a decent paying job, and coping with discrimination. The side effects of this kind of chronic stress is debilitating emotionally and physically and can result in serious health issues. I envisioned that this facility could be a community resource where people could learn about advocacy. I developed a mental health technician component for staff, so they could help people with the basic needs like finding housing or getting a job. This would help lower some of the stress levels so the people we served could get their lives on track. The clinic also focused on primary prevention, which for me meant keeping people from having mental breakdowns and helping them keep their lives together. I had to develop a community mental health education component where we did seminars, provided mental health education, and offered group counseling and therapy. We didn't offer specific family planning services, but all of the therapists and staff provided this type of counseling to women who needed it.

I formed a nonprofit organization to run the facility and hired a professional bookkeeper and accountant as well as professional psychiatrists and psychologists. I was able to get $2,000 in funding from Berkeley's Community Projects Office, which I had to fight hard for, because they didn't have a history of funding black student projects. I used these funds as seed money and then succeeded in getting additional funding from the City of Berkeley, as well as some other Bay Area cities and foundations.

At the time, my good friend Rudy Glover worked at the San Francisco Foundation and he helped me navigate my proposal through the Foundation's rigorous approval process, which resulted in my receiving a grant of $30,000. Several years ago Rudy died and his death really shattered me but I will never forget how he helped me get CHANGE started. In addition to the grant I received from the San Francisco Foundation, I was able to piece together about $100,000 from various fund-raising campaigns and donations. This gave me the capital I needed to start and sustain CHANGE, and I was able to build political support for the clinic and develop a strong Board of Directors. The clinic opened in 1974 in Berkeley with the help of two friends, Jaunita Papillion and Deborah Johnson. Jaunita was a psychologist who became the clinical director. Deborah was a social work student and later became director of children's services. Under their leadership, CHANGE flourished. We were able to raise enough money to hire folks to keep it going and provided about ten jobs, consultant contracts, and other forms of employment to the local community. It was a fulfilling and rewarding way to give back to the African American community. CHANGE survived until the early 1980s. Although I left to serve on Rep. Ron Dellums' (D-CA) Capitol Hill staff in 1975, I remained on the board at CHANGE until the end.

CHANGE was a model that gave people something to hope for, and much of our work was based on the same principles as the Black Panther *The Ten-Point Program*. Although I supported the work of the Black Panthers, CHANGE never received any direct support from the Panthers. Instead there was a synchronicity between the work going on at CHANGE and the stated goals of *The Ten-Point Program* which says:

We want completely free health care for all black and oppressed people. We believe that government must provide, free of charge, for the people, health facilities which will not only treat our illnesses, most of which have come about as a result of our oppression, but which will also develop preventive medical programs to guarantee our future survival. We believe that mass health education and research programs must be developed to give all black and oppressed people access to advanced scientific and medical information, so we may provide ourselves with proper medical attention and care.

The Panthers understood the poor living conditions in the black community and while eradicating poverty was a tough goal to accomplish, one way to chip away at it was by offering good quality health clinics and by preventing unwanted pregnancies, both of which were an issue that could be easily addressed. In my application to UC I stated that:

A clinical psychologist must speak out on every crime against humanity that has produced discontent, sick and frustrated individuals, whether that be through politics, development of programs, or helping effect change in the various social institutions which I see as responsible for this discontent. As a black woman living in a society such as this, I cannot see my job as totally one of a therapist because this would make my work individual rather than collective in nature. To quote psychologist Abraham Maslow, "Sick people are made sick by a sick culture; healthy people are made possible by a healthy culture. But it is just as true that sick individuals make their culture sicker and that healthy individuals make their culture healthier. Improving individual health is one approach to making a better world.

One health issue that I am committed to is the eradication of the worldwide HIV/AIDS pandemic. This disease is the greatest humanitarian crisis of our time and the vast majority of those affected by HIV/AIDS are living in Africa and the developing world, and women and children are the most vulnerable victims of this disease.

In the United States, the Centers for Disease Control and Prevention (CDC) estimates that for the first time in American history, more than 1 million people are living with HIV/AIDS. African Americans and other minorities have been disproportionately affected by the disease. For example, despite making up only 13 percent of the population, African Americans represent more than 42 percent of all people living with HIV/AIDS. However, in Alameda County the number of cases among women rose steadily from the 1990s through 2003, according to a 2005 HIV/AIDS epidemiology report from the Alameda County Public Health Department.

My efforts in promoting effective, bipartisan measures to stop the spread of HIV/AIDS and bring treatment to the infected has gained international attention and as the co-Chair of the Congressional Black Caucus Task Force on Global HIV/AIDS and as a senior Democratic Whip, I have played a leading role in the development of every major HIV/AIDS bill since I entered Congress. By working with my colleagues from both parties, I have introduced pivotal legislation to ensure the effective adoption and implementation of laws addressing the effects of the global HIV/AIDS pandemic. The legislative actions I have spearheaded have included H.R. 3519, the Global AIDS and Tuberculosis Relief Act of 2000, which represented the United States' efforts to fight HIV/AIDS and the related threat of tuberculosis. I wrote this bill with former Rep. Jim Leach (R-IA), a wonderful man and a moderate Republican who in 2000 chaired the House Banking Committee on which I served. This bill was signed into law by President Bill Clinton and created a World Bank AIDS Trust Fund, which was meant to serve as a new multilateral funding mechanism for programs that needed money for HIV/AIDS prevention and care and created the framework for what is now known as the Global Fund. My predecessor, Rep. Ron Dellums (D-CA), had had a similar idea that he called an "AIDS Marshall Plan." Rep. Jim Leach (R-IA) and I worked together to develop this landmark legislation, which incorporated many of the basic components of Congressman Dellums' visionary idea. On May 27, 2003, President Bush signed into law the President's Emergency Plan for AIDS Relief bill (PEPFAR), which I co-authored and which helped set up the $15 billion dollar Global Aids Initiative. I attended the signing of the bill where President Bush mentioned me in his "thank you" for the bill, and he said that the bill is part of the "moral duty" of the United States to act against a disease that has killed more than 20 million people worldwide. I am pleased that I helped renegotiate most of the bill's provisions when it came up for reauthorization in 2008 and especially pleased that we were finally able to get rid of the "abstinence-only" requirement.

I also worked on other important HIV/AIDS legislation in the areas of access to prevention measures, medication, and other treatment. So in recognition of the prominent role access to medication plays in extending the lives of infected people and in keeping families together, in 2001, I introduced H.R. 2069, the Global Access to HIV/AIDS Prevention, Awareness, Education and Treatment Act, and H.R. 1185, the Global Access to HIV/AIDS Medicines Act, which codified President Clinton's executive order to provide global access to HIV/AIDS pharmaceuticals and medical products by allowing countries with high HIV/AIDS rates to manufacture generic HIV/AIDS drugs and to exempt them from patent restrictions on life-saving HIV/AIDS drugs.

To protect vulnerable children and orphans in situations where their infected parents or guardians can no longer support them and to protect orphans who are infected, I got passed the Assistance for Orphans and Other Vulnerable Children in Developing Countries Act of 2004, which provided social, educational, and economic support for these children. In June 2006, I introduced a bill that would require the president to develop a comprehensive strategy to reduce the vulnerability of women and girls to HIV/AIDS infection in developing countries. This would eliminate the requirement that 33 percent of HIV/AIDS prevention funds be spent for "abstinence-only" programs. The Protection Against Transmission of HIV for Women and Youth (PATHWAY) Act of 2006, which I sponsored with the bipartisan support of 53 other members of Congress, would require the president to address 12 key issues that contribute to gender disparities in the rate of HIV infection. The key issues the Bush administration must address under the PATHWAY Act include the social and cultural factors which contribute to women's vulnerability: tribal and patriarchal traditions that historically have not allowed women to have a say in family planning and the decision to have more children; the fact that husbands and male partners can very often have multiple female sexual partners that result in transmission within entire families; the stigma of any woman refusing to have sex with her husband; lack of protection from the disease due to male refusals to use condoms or the lack of availability of condoms; lack of education about the disease for women and how to prevent its spread to their children; the stigma attached to HIV; and discrimination against women in nontribal countries that limits their ability to have access to protection. In many patriarchal societies women do not have a say over birth control or their own bodies, and they are often forced against their will to have sex with men who are infected with HIV/AIDS, often resulting not only in their own contraction of the disease but that of their unborn children. Much of the PATHWAY Act has been now included in the reauthorization of PEPFAR.

I see no reason why a person should be more vulnerable to HIV/AIDS because she is a woman, but the fact remains that women and girls in developing countries are bearing the brunt of the global HIV/AIDS pandemic. Our prevention efforts must be sensitive to the growing gender disparity and should focus on providing women and girls the education and resources they need to protect themselves. We know from the UN and World Health Organization's (WHO) *AIDS Update*, released in December of 2007, that every day, more than 6,800 new persons become infected with

HIV, usually because they don't have access to preventive methods of protection and that every day more than 5,700 persons die from AIDS, mostly because treatment services and drugs are inadequate or unavailable. This same report, pointed out that tragically, the part of the world suffering the most from the AIDS scourge is sub-Saharan Africa where the leading cause of death is AIDS. The 2007 WHO Update showed that just in 2007 about 2.5 million people worldwide were newly infected with HIV. It was estimated that there were about 33.2 million people worldwide living with HIV, and about 2.1 million people around the world had died from AIDS. Often the increases in cases of AIDS infections are among women and children who don't have the freedom to choose to abstain, which makes the whole "abstinence-until-marriage" approach not only irresponsible, but inhumane. In sub-Saharan Africa, the 2007 UN and WHO Update showed that almost 61 percent of adults living with HIV were women and that "90 percent of all HIV-positive children live in sub-Saharan Africa."

My work in the fight against global HIV/AIDS extends beyond my role as a legislator. I have urged organizations and local governments to recognize the growing HIV/AIDS crisis and have met with American and foreign dignitaries to find creative and alternative ways to combat the disease. I was an official member of the United States delegation at the United Nations General Assembly Special Session on HIV/AIDS in New York, and I have spoken about the need to establish comprehensive sex education programs to meet the needs of all people, regardless of their lifestyles, in a number of local and international conferences like the XV World AIDS Conference in Thailand. Since I entered Congress, I have been the only representative who has attended all of the international AIDS conferences. To reach across as many ethnic, age, gender, economic, and lifestyle barriers as possible, in March 2007, I invited Product Red founder, and U2 front man, Bono to tour Oakland to help raise awareness about HIV/AIDS and to help with public outreach. Bono (and his great and effective advocacy group, DATA) is known for his efforts to amass enormous amounts of medicine and money to combat HIV/AIDS in Africa, and this was one of the first times he had directed intense focus on the epidemic in the United States. Bono joined me and other community leaders for two hours in a meeting with HIV/AIDS service groups, clergy, and HIV-positive people at Allen Temple Baptist Church in East Oakland before speaking at a news conference where he called me a "lioness" for my efforts on behalf of HIV/AIDS patients. It is a humanistic imperative that individual civil rights protections be guaranteed. Major strides have been made, but cruel and insensitive discrimination toward people infected with HIV/AIDS still exists in our society.

In the past, many believed that HIV/AIDS was a disease that primarily struck the gay community and with some exceptions, the spread of the disease among gay men has been slowed but other issues have come to the fore that affect the civil rights of all people whose sexual orientation is different from heterosexuals, and I have attempted to address these issues. At the federal and state level, the lesbian, gay, bisexual, and transgender community (LGBT) is now the focus of several attempts to limit their rights and benefits as individuals and to enshrine discrimination into existing laws and policies, and even the Constitution. This kind of institutionalized bigotry is un-American and so wrong that it cannot be allowed to continue. I find it personally and politically important that we stamp out this kind of hate because my state of California leads the nation in same-sex couple households, and in my district, the city of Oakland is number two in the nation for the highest concentration of same-sex couple households in a large metro area. I applaud the California court decision allowing gay marriages. I strenuously oppose any efforts to marginalize this important part of my constituency and rather than seeking to divide us, our government and our leaders should be working to encourage greater tolerance and understanding. Loving, committed same-sex couples should have the right to be married, receive legal recognition of their marriage, and exercise all the legal benefits associated with their marriage. Of course because of the separation of church and state which I strongly believe in, religious denominations should not be required to marry anyone if it goes against their basic religious tenets. However for me, as a "secular" lawmaker, I cannot support laws that discriminate against anyone.

Any effort that seeks to create a narrowly defined legal definition of marriage that excludes same-sex couples should be opposed. Our Founding Fathers firmly embraced the concept of the separation of church and state and would be appalled that the Bible has become a right-wing religious tool used to make radical changes to the Constitution based on warped interpretations of the Bible and God's word. When I was in the California legislature during the early 1990s I wrote a bill called The California School Hate Crimes Reduction Act. It was vetoed twice by then Gov. Pete Wilson, and I am convinced that these defeats were due to lobbying by the Rev. Lou Sheldon, who is the chairman of the Traditional Values Coalition. Rev. Sheldon made sure that Gov. Wilson vetoed this bill because I included a provision that included "sexual orientation" in the nondiscrimination language. I refused to take this language out, built a strong bipartisan coalition throughout California and Gov. Wilson finally signed it into law.

People like Rev. Sheldon's intent and interpretation of the division between church and state can lead to only one conclusion— that because marriage and the definition of the term used by evangelicals is so strictly based on religion, it cannot be the basis for prohibiting any kind of marriage in the eyes of the law and the Constitution. Thus, same-sex marriage should be allowed without restrictions or any deviations from the marriage rights of heterosexuals. The Republican Party has become hostage to a very fringe element of religious fanatics, and these misguided evangelicals promote an agenda of intolerance that is anything but Christian in its attitudes. There are those who have gone so far to the right that many Republicans have begun to leave the party. One member's actions and words, in particular, addressed this very real conflict on March 30, 2005. That was the date that former U.S. Senator and Ambassador John C. Danforth, wrote an op-ed for *The New York Times*. Danforth, an ordained Episcopal minister, wrote eloquently about the issues of religion in politics, the ban on gay marriage, and myriad other issues related to the inherent conflict between political action and religious proselytizing when he stated that

> The problem is not with people or churches that are politically active. It is with a party that has gone so far in adopting a sectarian agenda that it has become the political extension of a religious movement.
>
> As a senator, I worried every day about the size of the federal deficit. I did not spend a single minute worrying about the effect of gays on the institution of marriage. Today it seems to be the other way around.

Some Republicans want government to stay out of people's private lives, until they decide that their interpretation of the Bible and religion should become the law of the land and then they want to have it both ways. You can't one day believe that religion and the affairs of government should be separate and that government should stay out of people's private lives and another day believe that the state can legislate a person's religious beliefs or sexual orientation based on religious dogma. As a black woman who was forbidden to attend public schools because of the color of my skin, I am especially troubled to witness this divisive, unfair, and un-American attack on the civil rights of our fellow citizens and my constituents. And as a Christian who was raised to believe in tolerance, respect, and justice, I am especially saddened to see animus and homophobia cloaked in religious terms. In line with that, same-sex couples should not be denied any of the same rights as heterosexual married and domestic partner couples.

The opportunity to adopt children and provide a loving home to boys and girls who may otherwise be left in foster care is among those rights afforded to heterosexual couples and should be available to gay and lesbian couples. Currently, federal benefits for individuals exclude gay and lesbian couples from receiving equal treatment under the law, and this is unfair and discriminatory. They should get the same benefits as heterosexual married couples. To that end I cosponsored legislation that would extend benefits to domestic partners, including the Family and Medical Leave Inclusion Act and the Domestic Partners Benefits and Obligations Act. The former amends the Family and Medical Leave Act of 1993 to offer employees the benefit of leave time to care for a same-sex spouse, domestic partner, parent-in-law, adult child, sibling, or grandparent if the same-sex spouse, domestic partner, parent-in-law, adult child, sibling, or grandparent has a serious health condition, or needs some other kind of care. The latter is important because it would provide benefits to domestic partners of federal employees who are not eligible for the same benefits as married couples. I also support the Clarification of Federal Employees Protection Act, which affirms that federal employees are protected from discrimination on the basis of sexual orientation and repudiates any assertion to the contrary. Another area where the rights of same-sex couples need protection, is in immigration policy. As a cosponsor of the Permanent Partners Immigration Act, it was my goal to ensure that same-sex partners of United States citizens and same-sex partners of lawful permanent residents should have the same immigration rights that legal spouses of U.S. citizens enjoy.

Unfortunately, discrimination based on sexual orientation takes on many guises, and discrimination and violence against the gay and lesbian community requires a vigorous response by the government that will protect the safety and dignity of each individual. To do this the federal definition of a hate crime should be expanded to include sexual orientation, gender, gender identity, or disability. This new definition will in turn require vigorous prosecution and harsher criminal penalties for those who willfully commit violence based on sexual orientation. The Local Law Enforcement Hate Crimes Prevention Act of 2005 provides federal assistance to states and local jurisdictions to prosecute hate crimes.

Yet another area of discrimination based on sexual orientation that I have diligently fought against is in workplace hiring. Basic protections against discrimination in the workplace based on sexual orientation are desperately needed because current federal law provides legal protection against employment discrimination on the basis of race, gender, religion, national origin, or disability but *not* on sexual orientation. Federal laws should be expanded to include protections to members of the U.S. military so that all who want to serve and are otherwise qualified may serve in the U.S. armed forces without fear of reprisal regardless of their sexual orientation. That is why I am a cosponsor of the Military Readiness Act, which would repeal the current Don't Ask, Don't Tell policy that has been a resounding failure and resulted in the loss of dedicated, talented, and experienced service men and women, which our military cannot afford. This bill would allow gay and lesbian service members to serve openly. I have witnessed great things, but I have also been saddened by humanity's ability to look in the other direction when someone is suffering. Seeing for myself how demoralizing poverty, discrimination, and the spread of HIV/AIDS can be, if we don't develop an organized and concerted effort to stamp out these ills of society we will doom future generations to hopelessness. I have come to see my work for reproductive freedom, education, and disease prevention as a calling and not just part of my role as a legislator. Like Esther, I want to be counted among the people who chose action over lethargy, who stood up for those who could not, and I want to be known as a person of tolerance, Christian charity, and sisterly and brotherly love. We can build a future where people are free to live their lives with the people they love without the fear of governmental interference, where children are brought into a world by loving parents who want them and can afford to give them a childhood filled with hope and opportunity. Yep, it seems like I'm always swimming upstream. It is difficult and often lonely, but for me it is the right thing to do and fulfills what I wrote in my diary as we left El Paso when I was 13 years old. And so, I really do stay pretty happy in spite of it all.

Notes

1. The statistics about abortion are a cautionary tale of what happens when legal abortions are not the law of the land. In March 2003, the Guttmacher Institute, a nonprofit organization dedicated to advancing sexual and reproductive health worldwide through research, policy analysis, and public education, published a report written by Rachel Benson Gold, titled *Lessons from Before Roe: Will Past Be Prologue?* According to Benson Gold's research, "Estimates of the number of illegal abortions in the 1950s and 1960s ranged from 200,000 to 1.2 million per year." She also discovered that "A clear racial disparity is evident in the data of mortality because of illegal abortion: In New York City in the early 1960s, one in four childbirth-related deaths among white women was due to abortion; in comparison, abortion accounted for one in two childbirth-related deaths among nonwhite and Puerto Rican women."

Gold's report also found that poor "women paid a steep price for illegal procedures." In 1962 alone, nearly 1,600 women were admitted to Harlem Hospital Center in New York City for incomplete abortions, which was one abortion-related hospital admission for every 42 deliveries at that hospital that year. In 1968, the University of Southern California Los Angeles County Medical Center, another large public facility serving primarily indigent patients, admitted 701 women with septic abortions, one admission for every 14 deliveries. More affluent women have always been able to find some doctor, who for the right price, will perform a "therapeutic" abortion in a hospital setting or in a safe and clean office and then disguise it as a necessary gynecological medical procedure. And if that wasn't an option, they could go overseas and pay for clean safe procedures there. Poor women were given short shrift and without any kind of money for medical care, pre-natal care, and abortions, they have died young, in childbirth, or from botched abortions. As Rachel Benson Gold stated in her March report for the Guttmacher Institute "The Supreme Court did not 'invent' legal abortion, much less abortion itself, when it handed down its historic *Roe v. Wade* decision in 1973. Abortion, both legal and illegal, had long been part of life in America. Indeed, the legal status of abortion has passed through several distinct phases in American history. Generally permitted at the nation's founding and for several decades thereafter, the procedure was made illegal under most circumstances in most states beginning in the mid-1800s. In the 1960s, states began reforming their strict antiabortion laws, so that when the Supreme Court made abortion legal nationwide, legal abortions were already available in 17 states under a range of circumstances beyond those necessary to save a woman's life."

Chapter Seven

Every great dream begins with a dreamer. Always remember, you have within you the strength, the patience, and the passion to reach for the stars to change the world.

—Harriet Tubman

Every day in America, more than three women are murdered by a boyfriend, husband, or intimate partner. These women's deaths at the hands of their loved ones belie the myths portrayed on television that women often are killed by strangers jumping them on the street or in random acts of violence. To cover it up and push the problem "under the rug" there are people who prefer to use the euphemism "domestic violence" rather than call this murderous act what it really is—a hate crime. This sort of crime is perpetrated against women and continues to be poorly addressed by the courts, the police, and government. By sanitizing the brutal nature of violence against women and giving it less offensive or less descriptive terms like domestic violence, we risk trivializing the danger to women and their children and downplay the seriousness of the statistics. Domestic abuse or violence is assault, battering, beating, rape, emotional and psychological torture, and murder. There are many myths about what constitutes domestic violence, and there are even those who say things like "it was just a slap or I just pushed her around, I didn't really hurt her." The constant fear and vestiges of emotional and psychological abuse leave silent scars that never completely heal. I know from personal experience how damaging this kind of violence is to women and children and the toll it takes on families because I am a survivor.

Some of the women in my family were victims of battered women's syndrome so I am intimately aware that this is not an easy problem to overcome or escape. My biological father, James Lewis, was violent, and he learned this from his father Walter, who abused his wife, my grandmother Maude. Each of my mother's three marriages were filled with physical or emotional abuse and the effect of being surrounded by men who were constantly belittling, hurting, beating, and demeaning women imprinted on my brain. This subconsciously sent me a message that, as a woman, I was of so little worth that I should have no expectation to speak my own mind, should assume that I didn't deserve a better life for myself, and that I should subjugate my feelings, goals, desires, and personal liberties to my husband or boyfriend. Domestic abuse is about total control over the victim, yet it's ironic that many batterers feel they are the victims and not the abusers. Because women are so devalued as human beings, male abusers have elaborate denial systems that are designed to justify or excuse their violent attacks. In some cultures, religion is used and quoted as justification. In others, it's tribal custom. In more industrialized countries like ours we trivialize or downplay the serious nature of any form of abuse by saying the abuse couldn't be that severe or the woman would have left. It's the same old "blame the victim" tactic used against victims of rape.

In my family, the Lewis men—my grandfather Walter, some of his brothers, and my father, James—shared the traits of having uncontrollable and irrational tempers that were often given as an excuse for their behavior. They justified their abuse by saying they were insanely jealous, and they often imagined their women were guilty of infidelities that they felt justified the way women were treated in the family. They never showed regret or remorse and were incapable of having normal, healthy relationships with women because of their abnormal possessiveness and need to have absolute control. To this day, my mother calls them all "animals," and we will never know when the generational abuse started, but I know for certain that my grandfather taught my father how to behave with women. My grandfather and grandmother Maude lived on their farm in Holland, Virginia, with their two children, my father, James Henderson, and his sister, Aunt Gwendolyn. In 2008 I gave the commencement address at my grandmother's alma mater, Elizabeth City State University, in Elizabeth City, North Carolina. My grandmother graduated in 1914, and I literally felt her strong, yet sweet spirit with me. Maude was not a woman who suffered fools gladly or put up with much from anyone. She made her own valiant attempt to stop the cycle from being handed down to another generation. For her the last straw came after Walter broke a broomstick over her head. Otherwise, she told me, she would have killed him had she stayed with him. She promptly took Walter to court on assault charges and used the still tender bruises from the broomstick incident as evidence against him. And it worked, because they were divorced not long after that. Thankfully, a few years after her marriage to Walter ended, Maude married Jo Howell, a strong loving man who was good to my grandmother and who I always called Granddad. The psychological damage to my father had already been done though. He grew up to follow in his father's footsteps. I guess growing up watching his father beat and debase his mother had instilled in him the same message—that husbands beat their wives, that was just how some of the Lewis men dealt with women in relationships.

My mother Mildred met my father when she was on her way to Washington, DC, to look for work during WWII. My aunt and uncle were living in Portsmouth, and she stopped over for a visit on her way to DC and that was when she met my father. My mother has told me how he used to slap her when she crossed her legs in front of men, how he would prevent her from going anywhere without him, and that she left him many times, only to return later. It took him trying to strangle her to death before she finally filed for divorce. Although she was pregnant with my sister Mildred at the time, she knew in her heart that if she hadn't left she would've probably ended up dead.

As is typical in violent crimes committed against women in the home, children watch and learn and then mimic their parents once they become adults. This kind of violence is also a form of child abuse because it's very damaging to a child's psyche to see their mother beaten and tormented. Often, boys grow up to be abusers, and girls become victims, destined to repeat the same mistakes in relationships. The same was true in my family and knowing my mother was treated as less than human took its toll on my self-esteem and made me fragile emotionally. But I was lucky that my first husband Carl wasn't anything like the Lewis men. We were young and immature but Carl never beat me, and he was a good man. When Carl and I got married, I was 16 and he was 19 and by the time I graduated from high school, Carl was in the military. Right after I graduated from high school, Carl was deployed to England and I moved there to join him, which was where we lived for two years. We were pretty happy in England, traveled all throughout Europe, had fun playing cards on base, and spent a lot of time visiting friends. Our first son, Carl Anthony, who we call Tony, was born in England on September 28, 1965, and after Carl's tour of duty was over, we moved back to the States and lived in Pacoima, California, until 1967. I soon was pregnant again, and our son Craig was born on November 2, 1966.

We were a struggling young family. Carl was going to school and working, and I was a 20-year-old mother of two, who was also working full time doing clerical work processing claims at the welfare office in Glendale. The thought that one day I could, and would, become a welfare recipient never even crossed my mind and would have shocked me at the time. Day in and day out I handled claims for hundreds of poor people in search of some kind of hope or way out of the dead-end road their life had left them on. Back then welfare actually gave you access to not just financial help but help with things like going to school, helping you find affordable housing and day care and welfare could, if used as a safety net, help pull someone out of poverty. I realized this by watching the steady stream of women and children that passed through the Glendale office's doors but I didn't interact much with our clients. Most of what I knew about them came from processing their paperwork. What this experience did do for me was give me empathy for the difficulties they were facing, and it made me sorry that with all of our wealth and power, our country still had so many poor women and children just struggling to survive, and I felt really sorry for them.

In 1967, Carl moved our family to San Francisco, which was where my father, Garvin lived with his wife Reiko. He was still in the Army at the time and was stationed at the Presidio and hired Carl to work with him in the communications center. He let us stay on post with him and Reiko until we could get an apartment of our own, which we eventually did. Our first little place was in a brand new building called Eichler Towers and within a year we were on the move again. This time Carl had gotten a job with IBM in San Jose, and we were able to buy our first house. This was the first house that we had ever owned, and it was so beautiful I couldn't believe that it was actually ours. I loved everything about it. It was new, it was large, and it was in a great location. Carl's job at IBM was only about four to six blocks from the house, but I wasn't so lucky with my commute. I still had to keep my job to make ends meet and that meant commuting to San Francisco. I worked as a statistical clerk for the state and my grueling commute left me little time to spend with my family because San Francisco was about 65 miles away. To make the commute I'd get up at 4:30 a.m., drive to the train station, catch the train, and then take a bus to be at work at 8 a.m. This long daily commute began to take its toll on me but we had to live where we did so that we could afford to buy a home.

That was the price you paid then and now for living in a great place like the San Francisco Bay area. But the inflated cost of living is out of control, and no one should be forced to make such long commutes to find affordable housing. In the Bay Area there are many residents who make the taxing 100-mile daily commute just so they can live where the rents are affordable or where they could purchase a home. This kind of drudgery lowers the quality of life and negatively impacts our lives in many ways. From the high gas consumption to get to and from work, to the impact of pollutants on the environment, to the added stress of the drive, it's the toll long commutes take on family life that are the most invasive and destructive. People shouldn't have to drive that far just to find a house they can afford. They should be able to live closer to their jobs and children's schools. The commute, day in and day out, certainly was influencing me in negative ways. The combination of the work commute and our weekly Sunday visits with Carl's parents at their farm in Atwater were making our schedules unmanageable. Like clockwork, every Sunday, Carl and I would drop the kids off at the farm, which was two hours away, and then pick them up the following Friday. With me working, we were able to save money and afford most things even a boat, but despite having achieved a fairly middle-class "white" life at a very young age, Carl and I could feel the stresses in our marriage.

We argued a lot and, in retrospect, I think that because we were so young when we got married, we were "playing house" rather than living like adults who knew what they wanted from their marriage and life together. Carl was a kind and gentle man and loved me. His only flaw was that he wasn't the kind of man with crazy issues, and his good nature left a crisis vacuum in my life. Children who grow up in challenging backgrounds are often crisis oriented and have a hard time coping with a lack of drama or emotional tension. This is a typical reaction for women who grow up knowing their mothers were physically and emotionally abused; we are unable to appreciate a good man and instead are drawn to a toxic relationship, but at least it's familiar territory. Carl was a good provider, husband, and father but that wasn't our problem, it was me. I was discontent with my suburban life and began to dislike and resent him for no reason. After we returned from England, it felt as if all of the excitement had gone out of our lives. I would spend hours watching television as if in a daze. At some point I realized that my life was at a standstill and that I needed to be doing something meaningful, but I wasn't sure what I could realistically commit to. I had a full-time job with a long commute and a husband and two small children to care for. I would have loved to jump into the thick of things and gotten involved in one of the many movements that were springing up around the country. I could have had my pick of issues from civil rights to women's rights, to social justice, and the anti-war movement.

Carl and I argued about the house and especially about my housekeeping and even though he only worked a few blocks away from home, he expected me to do all the cooking and keep an immaculate household. What he wanted was a traditional wife. Over time, the daily drudgery of a long commute and housework began to really take its toll on my attitude and on our marriage. I wanted my life to be about more than scrubbing bathroom tiles, wiping babies' bottoms, and commuting back and forth to San Francisco. Just getting another job wasn't going to fix the problem, but one night I had a glimmer of an idea. I longed to do other things, like go to college or get involved in a cause and I desperately wanted some kind of intellectual stimulation. The situation at home only made me feel angry all of the time. I know now that I was too immature to realize what a good husband and father Carl was and that we could have maybe worked things out if we had talked more and been honest about our goals and feelings.

I was totally frustrated living in the white, corporate, suburban world of San Jose and sometimes rather than board the train for the long commute home, I would stay in the city after work just so I could feel alive and be around invigorating company. I started spending more and more time in San Francisco because I wanted to be part of the energy and action of the city. The more I saw of San Francisco, the more I dreaded going back to the humdrum of suburbia. I got much more excitement than I ever would have imagined, and my entire future and my outlook changed on April 4, 1968. The day was coming to an end after one of my endless commutes, and when I arrived and got off the train, I got into my red and white Cutlass Oldsmobile and turned on the radio. And then I heard news that left me so stunned I just sat there staring at the radio dial in a state of shock. Dr. Martin Luther King, Jr. had been assassinated in Memphis, Tennessee. It was as if a huge boulder had been placed on my chest, and I couldn't move or breathe. How could this have happened? It was a crushing blow, and I was so overcome by sadness that it felt as if my heart would break.

The waste of such a precious life, taken in such a cowardly and violent way, made me feel like the world had just been turned upside down. I sat in the car without moving, listening to the news for about an hour. Dr. King's death was an epiphany for me. It made me realize that I was just going through the motions, that my life didn't have any meaning or relevance, from one day to the next, and that my routine was leading me down a path without much of a future. Every day was the same. I went to work, took classes at San Jose

City College when I could, took care of Carl, the kids, the house, and had little time left for Barbara the person. Who was I and what did I want to do with my life? That hour sitting in the car was life transforming for me because it was then that I decided my life was not very relevant. I knew I had to do something to deal with racism and injustice. In retrospect, I think Dr. King's death contributed to my divorce. His death reminded me of what I was not doing to make America better for my people.

I became agitated and restless after Dr. King's death and my marriage to Carl really began to hit rock bottom. We fought all of the time, I was miserable, and poor Carl didn't really understand why I was so unhappy. The breaking point of my marriage to Carl occurred when he decided he wanted to go to Jamaica for a vacation but I didn't. Rather than talk things out like adults, I refused to go so Carl ended up going by himself. While he was away, I moved out without telling him and took the furniture and my clothes, and left. My in-laws had just bought a nice farm in Cold Spring, Texas, so I put the kids on a plane and sent them there to stay with his parents on their farm. I then moved to San Francisco, got my own apartment, and ironically got a job with IBM. I don't remember how I first met my future husband Bill, but he ended up being yet another one of the reasons that I wanted to divorce Carl. As time went by I began to see more of Bill who was in the master's of business administration program at UC Berkeley. His life revolved around studying, hanging out with friends, and philosophizing about life, and I don't think he ever worked a day in his life but lived off of financial aid and scholarship checks. When we met he told me he was four years older than I was, and as I began to see more of him our relationship deepened. He called me his "chocolate angel" and the physical side of our relationship intensified. Not long after, I moved in with Bill and decided to go back to school full time and quit my job at IBM. I made the decision to have the boys stay with their grandparents in Texas during this period which, turned out to be a wise decision, because not much after I moved in with Bill he began to become abusive.

As our relationship progressed he became increasingly violent. He would hit me and when I threatened to leave him, he'd apologize, tell me how much he loved me, and beg me to stay. There were brief periods of calm in our relationship, but most of the time Bill beat and badgered me so much that my eyes were always swollen from crying. He kept telling me this would all stop once we got married. The fact that I stayed with this man let alone considered marrying him was a casebook example of battered women's syndrome. Living with Bill was like a brutal, cruel nightmare that had come to life from which there was no escape. He was so emotionally, psychologically, and physically abusive that during most of my time with him, my sons stayed with their grandparents. The few times they were around him have left them with horrible memories of the terror he inflicted on us. There were many instances and scenes of abuse but some stand out in particular. Like the year I planned a surprise birthday party for him and invited his friends and family. When Bill came home he was surprised. I thought that the party had gone well and that Bill had enjoyed having his family and friends over. All of that changed once everyone left because after the party, he began to savagely beat me and told me that if I could plan something like that behind his back, he knew that I was capable of sleeping with other men behind his back too. The sheer insanity of the situation, his unfounded accusations, and the violence made me hysterical, and I cried for hours afterward.

Later that night, Bill appeared to have repented, hugged me, and told me that I should take something to calm me down. I told him that I didn't want to take a pill and refused to take what he was trying to give me. This infuriated him and he began to beat me again, telling me that it wouldn't stop unless I took the pill he had for me. Finally, desperate to have the beating come to an end, I gave in and took the pill. He said that it was a tranquilizer but he had lied to me and it turned out that it was LSD. I began to have awful hallucinations and was seeing strange things and feeling completely out of control. While I was hallucinating I wrote a bizarre letter about Art Linkletter's daughter. For some reason I remembered that she had committed suicide on an LSD trip, and I felt that I needed to write about this. In the same letter I rambled on about weird things and also wrote I should trust Bill because I loved him and love was good for me. The LSD trip was horrible and was not an experience that I would have ever had if he hadn't beaten and tricked me into it. To make matters worse, Bill then gave me some Thorazine because he said it would improve the after effects from the bad LSD trip. I had no idea what I was taking or how I would react to it, but for several weeks afterward I had memory lapses that came and went. One day I went to go pick up my financial aid check, only to find that I had forgotten that I had already picked it up. While I was suffering these periods of memory loss, my younger sister Beverly got married and I was her maid of honor. My son Craig was the ring bearer in the wedding, and we drove from Berkeley to Pacoima, which is about six hours away, to go to the wedding and because of the memory lapses I don't remember anything about the drive and only vaguely remember the wedding.

You would think that after the beatings, being drugged, and Bill's lack of employment, I would have had enough and packed my bags. But my willingness to stay is an example of the sick dependency that occurs between women and their abusers. And the abusers always rationalize and make excuses because the beatings aren't their fault. They're the woman's fault. Of course, Bill told me the reason he was so possessive and violently jealous was because he loved me and wanted to marry me. I believed that if I loved him enough, then marrying him would stop the abuse and we would live happily ever after. To prove how much I loved him we dashed off to Reno and got married and then later had a Catholic Church wedding in Washington, DC, where he was from, so we could be blessed by the church and his family could meet me. We had a big wedding that all of his family attended. On my side my aunt's husband's family, the Franklins, who lived in Washington, DC, and Maryland, attended along with some of the members of the Lewis family on my father's side. My mother refused to come because she couldn't stand Bill, and my sisters couldn't attend either for a variety of reasons. They may not have approved of Bill but grudgingly accepted him as my husband.

I felt like the perfect bride. I was happy and felt beautiful in my wide, white, pleated chiffon pants, with a matching top and veil that covered my long black hair. When I look at the pictures from that day, I see a naïve and really pretty young woman and remember thinking at the time that now that we were married the abuse would come to an end. Unfortunately, marriage didn't help, and the violence got worse. Bill became more and more deranged, controlling, and paranoid as time went on. He was convinced that I was sleeping around and was always looking for ways to prove it. To search for evidence of my infidelity he was constantly badgering me. One day Bill found what he said was some "yellow hair" in the bedroom and accused me of having sex with our landlord who was a married, white man. To punish and control me for this he beat me up, and I couldn't figure out how a blonde hair had gotten into our bedroom. Later, I found a yellow mohair sweater, which was the source of this "stray" hair but he refused to believe this explanation. And as time moved on he became more and more irrational.

I got a part-time job at Far West Laboratory for Education, Research, and Development, was attending school, had brought the kids home from Texas, and was trying to survive my volatile relationship with Bill and applied for welfare. By this time my sister Mildred was also living in the area and had moved to San Francisco with her husband. After Bill and I moved to Berkeley, his physical and emotional abuse got worse and rather than just leave him outright, I would leave him and move in with Mildred and her husband for a little while and then move back in with Bill. This happened several times before I finally was able to gather up the courage to leave him for good. I don't remember what the final straw was that made me leave him. I just remember being fed up, piling my two kids, my clothes, my poodle Cognac, and a few other things into the car, heading to Mildred's house, and having my blue Volkswagen Bug break down on the Bay Bridge on the way there.

Looking back, I see now that I was repeating the typical patterns of women suffering from battered women's syndrome. I have come to believe that my dissatisfaction with my marriage and with Carl was that he was a decent man who was not an abuser, and I had been conditioned to expect abusive behavior. For him to fit the pattern, I think I exaggerated his flaws because I was unfamiliar with good men who didn't hit women. Instead, I was attracted to a man like Bill because he behaved like I had heard my biological father, James Lewis, behaved, and I was looking for a father figure to take care of me. This is typical of women like me who don't know how to accept love, respect, and tenderness. There were times I felt like God was punishing me for leaving a good husband like Carl and then marrying a man like Bill, because after I left Bill, he made constant threats, said he'd kill me, and also demanded I not go out with other men. His rage was beyond control, and I filed the paperwork for divorce. Not long after this I was reading the morning paper one day and came across an article about a man in Berkeley who had knocked on someone's door at 4 a.m. and asked the homeowner if his child could come out and play. When the homeowner refused, the intruder pulled a gun, the homeowner slammed the door, called the Berkeley Police, and when they arrived there was a shootout between them and the intruder. As I read further, I saw that the intruder who had fought police was my former husband, Bill, and he had been arrested. The irony was that the day of his shootout with the police had been the same day our divorce was finalized.

Over the years Bill's condition had obviously spiraled even further into mental illness, and his behavior had become progressively worse. Bill seemed to have lost touch with reality and after our divorce he wrote me a letter saying that he still loved me and that I was very naïve and would be used as a doormat by other people. He told me that his code word for me was WOTPFLG, "wise old tigers play foolish little games." None of his babblings made any sense, but his unpredictable behavior and his use of a weapon against the police terrified me. After his release from jail he was admitted to the Veterans' Administration psychiatric hospital in Martinez and somehow managed to find a way to call me from there a couple of times. This unnerved me and made me fear for my life and forced me to live in constant terror that he would somehow find me. One day out of the blue, I received a post card from him at the hospital and all it said was "WOTPFLG, Bill." After his release from the psychiatric hospital, Bill moved back to his hometown of Washington, DC. In 1975 when I moved to Washington to work for Cong. Ron Dellums (D-CA), I was constantly unnerved with being in the same city as Bill. Later, I returned to D.C. in 1998 after being elected to Congress, and each time I lived here I was always looking over my shoulder or afraid that he would show up on my doorstep with a loaded gun. Bill was convinced that he needed to kill me for what he thought was my infidelity and he sent me notes both times, which scared me to death. When I heard of Bill's death several years ago, I was sad and prayed for him, but I was finally able to sleep better at night knowing that he wouldn't appear on my doorstep. Although my experience was terrifying, sadly it is all too common in the United States, and the statistics on violence toward women has long-term effects on the entire family.

Abuse of women takes many forms and most often is kept a secret by the victims because they are ashamed, not just that they are married or living with an evil, disturbed, or violent person who abuses them, but because they feel or are taught that they did something wrong and somehow must deserve the abuse. Abusers often co-opt their victims into covering up the violence or beat their victims in places so that clothing covers the marks and bruising. The abuse takes the form of slapping, name calling, being burnt with cigarettes, kicking, punching, verbal, emotional, and psychological intimidation, control of the finances, abuse of the children, and frequently the punching or kicking of pregnant women's abdomens. When women attempt to escape, defend themselves, or defy their abusers, it can escalate the severity or savagery of the abuse and forces them and their children to live in a constant state of fear. Their every move is controlled and their lives are frequently spent isolated from friends and family under the domination of unpredictable thugs. Women in these conditions know that if they don't comply there will be reprisals and more severe punishment. Often leaving and not succumbing can mean death. The maelstrom of conflicting emotions, stress, fear, and heightened awareness, makes the long-term psychological effects more damaging than the actual physical abuse.

The longer a woman stays in an abusive relationship the more likely she is to develop a posttraumatic stress condition. Add to this the high incidence of rape, and it's amazing that more attention, funding, support, police protection, and legal remedies are not forthcoming. Violence toward women is one of our best kept family secrets, and it has become so commonplace that we are inured to it. Lest anyone think that this phenomenon affects one part of the population more than others, there is no one group that is exempt from this shameful problem. Crimes against women cross every religious, racial, political, educational, and socioeconomic line; it is unfortunately the one thing women have in common around the world no matter where they come from or what their background. It's shocking, that in a country like the United States where we have made so many strides forward for women's rights that we lag far behind other nations in devising remedies in both the public and private sectors. Instead, where we excel unfortunately is in the levels of violent acts perpetrated against women and girls. Entire fields of study in psychology and psychiatry have grown up around the phenomenon, and in the courts there is a plethora of case law centered on just this area of violent crimes. We have passed this behavior down to the younger generations and now battered women's syndrome is the patrimony we have created for our children. What makes battered women's syndrome so difficult to identify and treat is that it's a form of posttraumatic stress, and women who have suffered from its effects are often traumatized by long-term abuse that began when they were children. These women often grew up watching their mothers being abused and as adults they tend to fall into the same repetitive patterns in their adult relationships and with their own families. They have been systematically victimized for so long by severe violence that they are incapable of having normal relationships. Women in this situation go through two distinct cycles of abuse that are part of the reason escapes are so difficult.

Pervasive violence is cyclical, and it's the repeating patterns that create an internal script that each person carries around in her or his head. Each member of the family, abuser and victim alike, has a role to play and a script that tells them how to behave in relation to the other members of the family. This script plays itself out the same way each time and by its repetitive nature, despite the insanity of the situation, this familiar pattern is a source of comfort for generational victims of abuse. Children who grow up in severely dysfunctional and horrendous living conditions only know their own environment and have no other model to compare their experience to. So for them, the self-destructive and damaging patterns and relationships that they get involved with as adults are learned at such an early age that it is almost subconscious. They are aware that they are in pain but growing up in such chaos makes children seek order or try to make sense of their chaotic environment just so they can function. These women have generational and episodic cycles of violence that reinforce both the abuse and women's acceptance as victims. They submit because they don't have any other model for male-female relationships upon which to base their behavior.

Generational cycles of abuse are heartbreaking because the abuse is passed down from parent to child and breaking this cycle is difficult without significant intervention and long-term treatment. Episodic abuse reinforces the behaviors taught by parents and occurs in repeating patterns between a minimum of two family members but may include the entire family. This kind of abuse sends the message that what is learned from the parents must be the norm, because it's repeated in other relationships as well. Children naturally mimic and repeat what they see their parents do, especially in relationships. Sons who watched their fathers abuse their mothers or who were abused themselves often grow up to repeat the same patterns with their female partners and with their child, which is an example of generational cycles of abuse. Daughters, who tend to subconsciously seek out abusive men and become victims in virtually every relationship in their lives, are experiencing episodic cycles of abuse. Each person's place and role in the family is defined by the script they have in their head that shows them how to interpret signals given by other people, how to react to violence and abuse, and how to find surrogates for the key family players in other types of relationships. These family dynamics are repeated at work, among friends, etc. It's common for battered women to work for employers who exhibit many of the same personality traits as those of an abusive parent. This dynamic triggers a response and behavior that makes the workplace yet another incubator for negative power balances.

The episodic cycles of abuse create a constant state of anxiety and heighten "flight or fight" effects because there are periods when abuse lessens and decreases based solely on the abuser's whims and their will to dominate. This sort of violence is about one thing, ultimate control, and by keeping women on edge in fear of the next unprovoked episode of verbal or physical abuse, they are kept frozen and in denial that a recurring pattern exists. We have created entirely new generations of predatory males and victimized females. Whatever strides forward were made by women during the beginnings of the women's movement were taken backward by decades during the Reagan era. Since then there has been a backlash against strong, successful, dominant female figures, as in the reaction to women such as Sen. Hillary Clinton (D-NY) and media entrepreneur Martha Stewart, and a constant drumbeat of negative, insulting, demeaning, and stereotypical images, attitudes, and views about women have become accepted. Thanks to the way women are portrayed by politicians, the media, and the religious right, we have so devalued women and girls that we tacitly accept that sexual and physical harassment, violence, and intimidation are happening in elementary schools, middle schools, and high schools and only give lip service to doing anything about it. According to the National Domestic Violence Hotline, "1 in 5 female high school students reports being physically and/or sexually abused by a dating partner. Abused girls are significantly more likely to get involved in other risky behaviors, they are four to six times more likely to get pregnant and eight to nine times more likely to have tried to commit suicide." The National Domestic Violence Hotline reports that as many as "one in three teenage girls reports knowing a friend or peer who has been hit, punched, slapped, choked, or physically hurt by her partner." To gussy up this pervasive problem by using terms like domestic violence belittles how damaging violence is not just to the women being hurt but to their children, future generations, and our society as a whole. The high costs of this problem are not just in mental and physical damage, there are also negative financial repercussions according to the National Domestic Violence Hotline whose estimates are that "almost 1 million incidents of violence occur against a current or former spouse, or girlfriend per year." The Hotline also has found that "violence against women costs companies $72.8 million annually due to lost productivity, seventy-four percent of employed battered women were harassed by their partner while they were at work, and ninety-four percent of the offenders in murder-suicides are male." These statistics are disturbing, and our country's lack of response, compassion, or willingness to come up with remedies is deplorable. The courts and police don't provide adequate protection, remedy, or restitution for women and their children, and more shocking is the fact that the Hotline's statistics show that as few as "twenty-six percent of doctors report domestic violence incidents against women, and seventy-four percent of all murder-suicides involved an intimate partner (spouse, common-law spouse, ex-spouse, or boyfriend/girlfriend)."

My personal struggles and problems with generational and episodic violence have given me a perspective on the issue of violence against women and have compelled me to reach out to other families to confront the problems and help overcome the roots.

While in the California legislature, I authored many bills on domestic violence, including the Violence Against Women Act. I
will never forget participating in a women's caucus hearing at the
California Institution for Women in Frontera. We were at the
prison trying to get testimony from women who had killed their
spouses in self-defense. All of these women had been continuously
battered for years, and we were trying to get Gov. Pete Wilson to
grant them pardons. Well, during the hearing, an African American woman told her story, which was very similar to mine. All I
could think was "only by the grace of God" that I wasn't sitting
there in jail with them because they fought back, and I didn't.
There were press and cameras at the hearing. I broke down, ran out
of the hearing, and cried like a baby.

The statistics about this national epidemic are staggering, and
women of color bear a significant number of these incidences. According to a report published in the *Archives of Internal Medicine* in
1997, black women were the victims in 53 percent of the violent
deaths that occurred in the homes of female victims; 16 percent of
black women were physically abused by a husband or boyfriend in
a five-year period, according to a 1996 survey by the Commonwealth Fund. In 1998, a study that was tracked by the Annenberg
School for Communication at the University of Pennsylvania
noted that blacks see domestic violence as one of the most serious
problems in their community, and two of every five blacks said they
know a woman who was beaten by a man in the last year. Because
many of the women who are victims of this violence live in public
housing, I have also tried to make sure that they don't lose their
homes and end up on the street. One of the number one causes of
homelessness among women is the lack of safe havens, affordable
housing, and the flight from husbands that often means women end
up living on the streets with their children.

Victims of domestic violence should be protected from eviction from public housing, and to ensure this I recently pushed through committee an amendment to the Housing Affordability Act enacted by former President Bill Clinton. This Act included what was referred to as the "one-strike policy," which allowed authorities to evict tenants if they or anyone living with them were caught selling or using drugs on or near public housing units. The Lee amendment is designed to protect victims of domestic violence who live in public housing or receive Section 8 assistance by prohibiting public housing authorities and Section 8 landlords from evicting tenants for the criminal activity of their household members and guests if the tenant was a victim of domestic violence, to respond to cases where victims of domestic violence were threatened with eviction because of the disturbance to other neighbors caused by domestic violence, and the second part of the amendment would allow public housing authorities to evict individuals for domestic or dating violence as opposed to evicting the entire household.

We have much work to do to make families stronger, healthier, and safer, and it must begin with the parents. Children learn from the models that they grow up with, and if they only know power, control, violence, and fear then the toxic ways they relate to all people, not just their family members, will ripple outward into society. We have to teach families suffering from generational abuse new ways of expressing their anger, frustration, pain, and suffering and give them coping mechanisms that encourage communication, self-esteem, and love. We have to empower young girls so that at any age they will automatically reject and report any incidence of abuse or violence and not be submissive, compliant, or silent when threatened, coerced, or attacked. As much as I support the principle that nations should always work to find peaceful resolutions to their differences, I firmly believe that nonviolent solutions to domestic disputes should be a cornerstone of family life. A family that can work through differences without resorting to angry words and actions creates members of the global community who will take the same approach to solving conflicts which extend across political and religious borders.

Let us all take the words of Proverbs 15:1 to heart, "A soft answer turneth away wrath: but grievous words stir up anger."

Chapter Eight

You just need to be a flea against injustice. Enough committed fleas biting strategically can make even the biggest dog uncomfortable and transform even the biggest nation.

—Marian Wright Edelman

Having gone from living with violent abuse to organizing a sit-in at the president's office at Mills College, and working with the Black Panther Party, it's hard to believe that such distinctly disparate aspects of my life could have occurred so closely together. They may seem like worlds apart from each other, but they are as much a part of me and the person I have become, as my faith in God. No one ever imagined the horror occurring in my personal life. The public saw a young idealistic woman with a big Afro involved in many community activities while raising two boys. But when the doors were closed, it was hell. Mills is a women's college that provides a nurturing and supportive environment for women to learn to stand on their own and discover who they want to be. Going to Mills was one of the best things that ever happened to me because it was a safe environment that encouraged me to become an independent, free-thinking woman for the first time in my life. At Mills I was just another young woman finding what my strengths were on a beautifully calm and healing campus where the study of liberal arts has put them in the forefront of women's colleges. The diversity of the student body gave me a chance to develop leadership skills, filled me with confidence, and helped shore up my usually poor self-esteem. By being around women from so many backgrounds I gained insight into the importance of inclusion and collaboration, and I became proud of my African American heritage through my involvement with the Black Student Union. This time on my own gave me a chance to just be Barbara and not someone's wife, mother, daughter, or girlfriend and when I joined the Black Student Union (BSU) it changed my life for the better.

By getting actively involved in politics and the BSU, I was empowered to fight not just for myself, but for women, and especially for black people. The Mills campus and the BSU were a fertile training ground that allowed me to develop important organizational and political strategizing skills, eventually leading to my tenure as president of the BSU for two years. This lush college nestled in the middle of Oakland has become a beacon for women and over the years has expanded its role in the local community. When I was a student there, it had no commitment to the city of Oakland itself and when I ran for BSU president, I strongly encouraged students to get more involved in community activities to become a part of a vital link to the local people and their needs. Once I was elected, I was able to get students to volunteer to help with Black Panther Survival Programs, worked to get the college to donate some money to some worthy community groups, one of which, somewhat ironically was the Black Panthers. The leadership skills I gained there would serve me in good stead later in life so you can imagine how touched and surprised I was when Mills College announced the funding of a $2 million endowed chair at the college called the Barbara Lee Distinguished Chair in Women's Leadership. According to Mills, this endowed chair was established in recognition of my outstanding leadership, conviction, and courage in politics, policy, and human rights, and the chair will be held by a national expert in her field who is also a recognized scholar.

When I was blessed with such an extraordinary symbol of respect the President of the college, Janet L. Holmgren said that

> The Barbara Lee Distinguished Chair in Women's Leadership honors the extraordinary public leadership of Congresswoman Lee and her exceptional work across the borders of ideological and cultural difference. This Chair will bring an exemplary scholar to teach and provide visionary leadership within Mills' dynamic multicultural environment.

For me, this distinguished honor is not about me personally, but about Mills College as an institution of higher education that inspires women to shake things up, to challenge the status quo, and to recognize the absolute requirement for academic excellence. This chair is part of the process of societal change and reminding women what our great sister suffragette Susan B. Anthony said, "failure is not an option," which is on a mug I drink coffee from at home in the morning which is inspiration for the day. That is why we have a phenomenal woman, Nancy Pelosi, as Speaker of the House. We should have 250 women in the House of Representatives instead of 73 and 50 in the Senate instead of 16.

To have come from being a student at Mills to having a chair named in my honor was quite a ways from my tentative first steps there in the 1970s. When I began my work with the BSU I realized that I had to do everything I could to emphasize the importance of understanding where we came from but, more importantly, who we were as women of color. One of my priorities as president of the BSU was to empower black students to demand that the college offer classes and activities that had a focus on issues relevant to us and our local community. As part of this process, it was essential that black history be taught as part of the curriculum and also be included as part of the semester abroad programs offered at the school. Mills had a January term that offered students the opportunity to participate in overseas independent study courses, the problem was that not one country in Africa was part of the overseas program, which left black women interested in African culture and history without any options. I readily admit that I am stubborn, and it was my determination to see this happen that made me keep fighting to get this program established as an accredited study course in Africa. If there could be programs in places like Europe, South America, and Asia there shouldn't be any reason that Africa not be included. To force the school to address the issue, I organized other students to help me fight to get the program instituted, which finally happened. The problem then became the funding for the trip to Ghana, which was the country we selected. Many of the African American students were receiving financial aid. Well, I helped raise money for the students from outside the college and we were down to $700 remaining for one student who wanted to go. I asked the college to make a $700 donation to the trip, and the help was refused. So I organized a sit-in at the late President Wert's office to demand assistance. President Wert eventually capitulated, and we were able to send our first group of 16 or 17 black students to spend their January term at the University of Legon, in Accra, Ghana. Unfortunately, I wasn't able to go because I couldn't leave my two sons behind for such a long time, and I certainly couldn't take them with me. But I believed so strongly in the exposure that this semester would provide a black student, that I ended up giving my slot to another student. I'm glad that someone was able to have the experience of a lifetime, even if it wasn't me. Mills was not just a place where I learned about my own strengths, skills, limitations, and goals, it was also an incubator for women's causes and it was while at Mills that I met a woman who would fundamentally alter forever my vision of women and people of color and their role in politics. It was while at Mills that I met and worked on Shirley Chisholm's presidential campaign. She was from Brooklyn, New York, and later became the first African American woman elected to Congress, which is how I first met Rep. Ron Dellums (D-CA), from Oakland. At the time he was the first African American in the House of Representatives elected from northern California. He became my mentor and role model and was so impressed with my work on the Chisholm campaign that he offered me a summer internship in his congressional office in Washington, DC, which I gladly accepted.

When I arrived in Washington, the Watergate scandal was in full swing and the city was constantly abuzz with breaking news reports about yet another "dirty trick" played by the Nixon White House. The proceedings of the House Judiciary Committee hearings were televised and broadcast around the country, and from time to time I was lucky enough to sit in on a hearing and watch history unfold before me. It was disquieting and humbling to witness the way the Constitution and system of checks and balances actually worked and to know that our country was capable of removing a seated president in a peaceful and legally sound fashion without the threat of a military coup or government takeover. When the House Judiciary Committee charged him with "high crimes and misdemeanors" in its bill of impeachment, it didn't matter that he made no confession and merely acknowledged that some of his judgments "were wrong." The American people knew that when it mattered, the members of the House had the courage to follow both the spirit and the letter of the laws of our country and do the right thing.

I distinctly recall President Richard Nixon's resignation and watching the helicopter through the office window in the Longworth House Office Building on Capitol Hill. As the helicopter flew over Washington, I felt sad that he had dragged our country and the presidency down into such a morass of illegal and despicable behavior, but I felt like it was in some way a day of reckoning for America. I was glad that we could finally get down to the business of democracy and put the scandals and abuses of the corrupt Nixon regime behind us. He had left the presidency in disgrace and in the process had eroded our country's faith in its leaders and sullied the power and prestige of the presidency. Our democracy was a little less for wear, and the office of the president had gotten tarnished. But I knew that our Constitution was intact and that the system of checks and balances had prevailed over an imperial presidency, despite Nixon's efforts to do otherwise. This catharsis was an important part of the healing process that would take years, and it now seems that we must again take this path if we are to right the wrongs left behind by the Bush administration.

What is especially chilling about the actions taken during Bush's two terms is not only the complete disregard for the law and the American people, but the similarities between the imperialistic styles of management, the control of the media, the repeated lies told to the American public, and the predilection for cover-up. Nixon was charged with the cover-up of Watergate crimes and that he misused government agencies such as the FBI, the Central Intelligence Agency, and the Internal Revenue Service. Bush continued this legacy, taking many steps further and making a mockery of what our Founding Fathers stood for and wanted for the future of our people. Bush did many of the same things as Nixon, including spying on Americans, illegally tapping phones, and allowing American soldiers to die based on lies about enemy strengths and capabilities. The Bush administration took things much further and imprisoned American citizens and other foreign nationals without due process, labeled people, without evidence or proof of crimes, as enemy combatants thus allowing them to be tortured and imprisoned against their will in secret prisons without any chance for access to their accusers or their families, and in eight years made his entire administration a cadre of warmongers and prevaricators bent on dismantling government in the name of smaller government. In reality, Bush and Cheney created the largest, most inefficient bureaucracy in history only to have it staffed by supposed antigovernment Republicans whose real agenda is to bankrupt the government. Bush and Cheney and their cohorts in the cabinet, elsewhere in the administration, and in consulting organizations like Blackwater, have been fleecing our country to line the pockets of criminally negligent and financially corrupt corporations like those headed by their friends, such as Halliburton.

After I graduated from Berkeley in 1975, I returned to the Capitol and became a full-time member of Dellums' staff, and it was an amazing time to be working for Congress. Our country was reeling from the aftermath of the Watergate scandal and still trying to come to terms with the end of the Vietnam War. The civil war in Nicaragua and the fight with the Sandinistas for control was front and center, and the departure of Old World colonial powers in many countries in the Third World had left economically and politically unstable countries behind in their wake. As a result Africa, Asia, and South America were experiencing conflict and strife and many Third World nations became havens for ruthless dictators and military juntas and ethnic and tribal tensions erupted into bloody genocides. The United States was forced to grapple with our perceived role as global peacemakers and protectors of human rights.

During the eleven years I worked for Dellums, I rose to become one of his top assistants and loved working for him on the Hill because he wasn't just a mentor to me, he was also a leader and a black man who was not afraid to stand up for what he believed. There were few others in his class that had so much charisma and conviction. Rep. Dellums (D-CA) was well-known for his opposition to the war in Vietnam and for military buildups, and he always argued that our tax money would be better spent working for peace and justice. His work to end apartheid in South Africa was groundbreaking, and he was able to successfully override President Ronald Reagan's veto of the Comprehensive Anti-Apartheid Act of 1986,

which called for a trade embargo against South Africa and immediate divestment in that country by American corporations. I am
proud that I was able to play some part in helping him achieve
these important steps, and it was from him that I truly learned
about standing up for what you believe in and for fighting for your
convictions. His courage and ability to take the moral high ground
and to follow a path alone guided me later in my own struggles to
do what is right rather than what is expedient. After leaving Dellums' office in 1987, I took a break from politics for a few years and
started my own facilities management company, which I ran for
more than a decade. By the time I sold it, it had grown to 500 employees. I was very proud of this company which I named after my
grandfather and called it the W. C. Parish Co., DBA Lee Associates
after the hundreds of jobs we provided for many people. It was a
family-run business and the chair of my board, a Morehouse College alumnus and successful businessman, Louis Barnett, helped
make it a positive, yet unbelievably challenging experience. However, I continued to work as Ron's fundraiser and got very involved
with the Rainbow Coalition, headed by Rev. Jesse Jackson.

The East Bay is unique because it is diverse, forward thinking,
and one of the most progressive places in the country. It is a place
that I am proud to call home, and importantly for me, it's a place
that I would be proud to represent as an elected state representative. Knowing that the call to re-enter politics couldn't be kept at
bay any longer, I decided to run for the California State Assembly
from the then-13th Assembly district. I put together a campaign
and was elected in 1990 and served as a Representative until I was
elected to the senate in 1996 where I would serve as the first black
woman from northern California to serve in the State Senate. During my tenure as a California legislator, I worked with Republican
Gov. Pete Wilson and formed a successful relationship that resulted
in my sponsoring 67 bills and resolutions that were passed by the
legislature and signed by him into law. This legislation addressed a

broad spectrum of community concerns, including public safety, education, women's issues, environmental protections, labor, health, and legislation designed to provide health care for California's uninsured children.

It was while I was still in the Senate in the California State Assembly that I one day received a phone call from a reporter telling me that my good friend and mentor Rep. Dellums (D-CA) was giving up his seat for personal reasons. I had no idea that he was thinking of leaving Washington at that point and was surprised that he was doing so because if he resigned in the middle of his term, there would need to be a special election. Recognizing that this was an opportunity that I wouldn't have twice, and knowing that raising funds on such short notice would be difficult, I made the difficult decision to run for the seat. I knew that a congressional race is much more expensive than a state campaign and that I had almost no time to do any fund-raising. Nonetheless, by the time the special election was held in April of 1998, just four short months after the Congressman's announcement, I had raised enough money for the campaign so that I could succeed him in the United States House of Representatives. That year I had three campaigns—the special election in April, the Democratic primary in June, and the general election in November.

I was proud and honored when Cong. Dellums (D-CA) endorsed my candidacy and literally handed me a symbolic baton at an election campaign event. He was very supportive of my campaign, and it meant a lot to me personally as well as politically. Ron and I have worked well together over the years and we shared similar ideologies, and I knew the constituents well from my time on his congressional staff.

Over the years I have had my share of critics and among them there are those who call me a radical intending to use the word as a slur and an insult. Well, if being a radical means someone who works to make liberty and justice for all a reality, then call me a radical. If a radical is a person committed to protecting the planet or wanting every man and woman to have access to good paying union jobs with benefits and want all children to have access to quality public education, then what is wrong with being a radical? I guess with things so bad for so many people, it is radical to just want a decent quality of life for everyone.

The people in my district are very committed to an agenda of peace and justice and have for years provided me with support and assistance. They have always encouraged me to fight for what is right and their issues have been my issues, such as getting the U.S. troops out of Iraq. What has been most disturbing are the people who have attacked me personally or who have made threats on my life and safety as a result of my "No" vote against giving the president unlimited power to go to war. The repercussions and long-term effects of that day were felt by many people, including my Chief of Staff, whose cousin was one of the people who tragically perished in the fields of Pennsylvania on ill-fated Flight 93. Despite whatever personal challenges I had to face in those tumultuous days I knew that someone had to be objective and take a longer view of how this decision would affect our country in the months and years ahead. I owed it to myself and my constituents to caution that we should not let our desire for vengeance lead us down the path of becoming the evil we deplore. As a result of my stand, I received thousands of hate letters and e-mails and received so many death threats that the Capitol Police recommended that I have protection. The fact that fellow Americans could hate me enough to want to kill me was terrifying, and it only proved how easily dissent and debate can be stifled and how our democracy can be quickly eroded during a national security crisis, when just the opposite should be true. I resented the invasive necessity of having bodyguards around me and the various ways it disrupted my life and freedom, but I will always be grateful to the Capitol Hill Police for protecting me. After working so hard my entire life to be an independent woman who refused to live in fear, being under guard day and night was very disconcerting for me. For months, I couldn't go anywhere without a security detail, and the feeling of constantly being watched was nerve-wracking. It was extremely difficult to have any semblance of a normal life knowing that there were people who were "out to get me" and that there were other people ready to give their life to protect me.

One of the greatest challenges of being a member of Congress is that we are required to think on several levels at once: locally, nationally, and globally. What kept me sane and fortified me during this volatile time was the knowledge that I was doing the work that my constituents wanted me to do, that I created space for the voices of peace in our own country and throughout the world, that I represented their wishes, and that I had brought millions of dollars into my district to help it become more viable. I have pushed for successful strategies to combat AIDS/HIV on the local level; better access to our ports; access to affordable housing; and federal funding for our schools, cities, the county, and nonprofits.

At the national level, I have always supported a compassionate budget because the amount of poverty found in America is astounding. We have incredible resources, wealth, and a population that is able to be educated and is surrounded by prosperity. It is the part of the population that is left behind during prosperity that I fight for the hardest. I am always working to ensure that America's wealth is shared by all because it's wrong that even one penny of our tax dollars should go to fight wars that have no end in sight. We should be using our resources to aid the disadvantaged, and if we are going to go into debt for anything, it should be for humanitarian reasons and not for military engagements. My resolution, to cut poverty in half in ten years, passed unanimously in 2008.

We have a responsibility to the international community as well and our country has been blessed with intangible resources beyond compare. We have an obligation to share our knowledge, technology, and advances in medicine and science with nations that have not been as blessed as ours. We are the United States of America, and for more than 200 years our country has stood for peace, liberty, and the right of people to self-determination. It is not our place to impose our views onto our allies with the threat of reprisal if they don't agree with our goals and beliefs. Under the Bush administration we became oppressive, threatening thugs who told our friends that our insular view of world politics was the only view and that there would be consequences for not following our lead. There are few examples of such a unilateral view becoming the overriding thesis of our foreign policy, and as a result of our occupation of Iraq and Afghanistan, our threats toward Iran, and our castigation of countries like France who opposed our tactics, we have become diplomatic and political pariahs around the globe. We have not learned that we cannot force feed democracy down the throats of other nations and that if we are to achieve global peace and economic stability we must first adhere to our own principles of the rule of law. The hypocrisy and abuse of trust that were characteristic of George Bush's two terms have cost us dearly in terms of the lives lost, our loss of faith in our own government, our loss of respect worldwide, and in our financial losses of trillions of dollars, the debt for which will have to be borne by our children, grandchildren, and future generations. Just consider for moment what we could have accomplished if we had listened to our conscience and not George Bush, who constantly said that we didn't have the money to provide health care to the 43.6 million uninsured? Think what life-changing events could have occurred if we had committed the hundreds of billions of dollars we have spent on the war in Iraq to active diplomatic engagement.

The United States has had its share of shameful history, political and financial scandals, and embarrassments as a nation governed by laws. We tolerated slavery, prohibited women from voting, have engaged in dubious military exercises, but we can overcome this past and I have faith in our people and our system of government;

it's our core values that bring us together and which give us the fortitude to work together to achieve greatness. I know that we can overcome any obstacle and that the scars of war and unrest can be worked out because, despite being under attack from all political sides, even after my own controversial vote, I received thousands of e-mails and letters of support, including campaign donations, which was totally unexpected.

I have won all my bids for re-election with an over 80 percent margin but if we are to avoid having another presidency like Bush's foisted upon us, we must closely examine our electoral process. The voting problems that plagued Florida, Ohio, and parts of other states in 2000 and 2004 are just the tip of the iceberg. In many states people of color have been disenfranchised by illegal means. Polls have been moved or closed without notifying the voters, or not enough polls were opened and people were forced to stand in line for up to ten hours just to vote. I hope the challenge to the tainted electoral votes in the 2000 presidential election brought much needed national attention to this shameful state of affairs. I was surprised to see a clip of me in Michael Moore's *Fahrenheit 9/11* when I helped lead the protest on the floor of Congress against the Florida vote in 2000. I will never forget that moment in my life. I delayed my departure for a visit to Taiwan and stayed in Washington, DC, for the Saturday morning session where Vice President Al Gore, whose election was just stolen, presided over the session. He didn't really want us to protest this, but I sensed that deep down inside he was pleased. Like the few members who stayed to join in this effort, I decided that this was more than just about Al Gore. It was about a stolen election and folks' democratic rights being snatched from them. I was very dismayed that we could not find one member of the United States Senate to stand with us in this protest.

As one who got involved in politics as a young student, I have always worked to involve young people in electoral politics, whether it was when I chaired the California Rainbow Coalition, whose founder, Rev. Jesse Jackson, Jr., has been a remarkable leader and a powerful voice for peace and justice, chaired the Northern California Young Democrats, worked with the hip hop community on voter registration and voter education efforts, or was part of the congressional Younger Voter Project. And I had an amazing time working with young people in my district on many campaigns, including the Obama for President campaign, which thanks in large part to the young people's active involvement, turned out 62 percent for Barack in my congressional district on Super Tuesday 2008.

There have been enough studies done to warrant a prediction—our young people face a 40 percent benefit cut in Social Security, which is not what we want for our nation. The alarmist predictions made by Bush were not borne out by the reality of how Social Security functions—the system is not in crisis as he suggested, but it does face some challenges. The source of those challenges comes from the misappropriations made from the Social Security Fund that have been needed to cover other programs because the Bush people and Republicans in Congress continued to dole out corporate welfare and tax breaks as well as tax cuts to the most wealthy people in our country.

In a country where roughly 1 percent of the population controls 90 percent of the wealth and the numbers of people falling onto the poverty rolls or even worse, below them, are at an all-time high, we should have suspected foul play. George Bush and Dick Cheney came from that wealthy 1 percent, so when he suggested that we privatize Social Security, give tax cuts to the wealthy in the midst of an economy stagnant with high unemployment, a housing market in failure, and a dollar worth little on foreign markets, not to mention a debt spiraling out of control, we should have shouted No! We will not help the rich get richer while the poor get poorer. When the Bush administration passed a $1.6 trillion tax cut that primarily benefited the wealthy, it neglected to find other methods to pay for Social Security due to the ensuing loss of revenue. The proposal to privatize Social Security does absolutely nothing to extend the life of the program or save it from an early demise. For millions of Americans, Social Security is the only protection against the shackles of low lifetime earning, the financial hardships related to death or disability, the danger of poverty in old age, and the uncertainty of inflation. Privatization undermines these protections and adds one more problem that workers would have to worry about—individual financial risk. Between March 2000 and April 2001, the S&P fell by 28 percent. Imagine the devastating effect this drop in the market would have had on the incomes of people who depended on Social Security as their sole source of income. If Social Security had been privatized, retiring workers who had their individual accounts invested in a fund that mirrored the S&P 500 would have had 28 percent less to live on for the remainder of their lives. A government-secured Social Security program provides guaranteed life-long benefits. No matter what the stock market does on any given day, your benefits are not affected.

Although the young may not quite understand the importance of preserving Social Security they did understand the importance of finding a candidate in the 2008 presidential campaign who inspired them to action and for whom they could vote. Support for Barack Obama for president was strong among all age groups and ethnic lines and young people in particular responded to his message. Like many of our nation's people, I endorsed Sen. Barack Obama (D-IL) for president, in part for his commitment to engaging the youth vote. For me, the movement he built with young folks of all races was essential, and I liked his message of fundamental change, which was as close to a revolutionary message as we have had in decades. I believe he represents a bridge to the future and that he embodies the hope and new direction our country so desperately needs. I am convinced that he can be a real agent of change. I also think he is straightforward clear. I was Sen. Obama's Western Regional co-chair, and on his behalf I participated in rallies, phone banking, and behind-the-scene advising on issues and politics. I organized "Team Lee" volunteers to go to South Carolina and Texas to campaign and support his presidential bid. I went to South Carolina, Houston, North Carolina, and Indiana and spoke on his behalf at churches and rallies, attended volunteer campaign events, and did radio and TV interviews. In addition to helping Sen. Obama (D-IL) campaign in California I also attended several debates—the Howard University debate on issues important to the African American community, the George Washington University debate with the topic of faith and politics, and also the Congressional Black Caucus Institute's debate in South Carolina and the California Democratic Party debate in Los Angeles. I also attended the rally in Washington, DC, on the American University campus where Sen. Ted Kennedy (D-MA), Cong. Patrick Kennedy (D-RI), and Caroline Kennedy all publically endorsed Senator Obama (D-IL).

Barack and I spoke on several occasions before my endorsement and in our conversations we discussed his position on the war and other issues as well as my history of not endorsing and working in many presidential primary campaigns. I am very careful about making endorsements and even before I was elected to Congress, I was reluctant to work for candidates I did not believe in. For the most part I told Sen. Obama (D-IL) that I had only worked on two presidential campaigns, first for Rep. Shirley Chisholm (D-NY) and then Rev. Jesse Jackson. I told him that my campaigning for them wasn't because they were black but because they were progressive and spoke clearly about their positions on issues and took on the status quo. They just happened to be black. He told me that I knew already what I had to do and that my reputation was such that I had to do the right thing. Barack Obama was and is an inspiring man, and he touched a chord with young people. I have a lot of hope for the future because of what I know about our youth. They became and continue to become more involved in politics now because they see a glimmer of hope and want to be part of the change they desperately want. And with an aging population and the sheer numbers of baby boomers that will be retiring, they will have to be creative problem solvers and will have to make tough decisions if they are ever to deal with the long-term financial repercussions of the Bush administration's tax cuts for the wealthy and its attempts to privatize Social Security.

In the 2008 race for the presidency, Sen. Hillary Clinton (D-NY) was a great candidate and I liked her positions on HIV/AIDS, women, and healthcare. I greatly admired her strength; it was difficult for a woman to have run for president because there is still so much sexism surrounding women in politics. We knew that California would be a tough state for Sen. Obama (D-IL). The Clintons had a long history of involvement and support in California. However, Barack won 10 congressional districts in California, and my congressional district had the highest voter turn-out for Sen. Obama (D-IL), around 62.4 percent, and we actually picked up four more delegates due to reaching the 58 percent threshold for an additional delegate.

We need more women to do work at the community level, as elected officials, in the charitable world, and in the corporate world, and we need them to bring men along to help them because we are at a critical moment in our democracy. The Bush administration single-handedly reversed years of progress in the areas of regulatory laws, consumer and patient protections, financial and social welfare programs and safety nets, international peace and diplomacy, the fight against HIV/AIDS, women's rights, human rights, and he had a vision of the world that was viewed through the scope of a rifle. Under George Bush our country was no longer recognizable as one of compassion, understanding, and freedom and unfortunately our foreign policy became one that embraced first strikes. We were on the wrong course, but just as I have had to endure tremendously sad and devastating personal challenges during my elected public life and have had to develop coping mechanisms and ways to rise above these challenges, I will continue to try to find ways to deal with the trauma that the Bush administration has had on millions of lives here at home and throughout the world.

Nothing could be more dangerous than a continuation of these policies and actions and so I was also concerned about Sen. John McCain (R-AZ) as a candidate during the 2008 presidential race. I have worked very hard to be sure that he would not be elected as our next president. A President McCain scares me. I believe he means for us to be in Iraq for 100 years. I don't think he has a clue about poverty, public education, housing—all of the domestic quality-of-life issues that the Latino, African American, Asian/Pacific American, and Native American community see as priorities. I don't think that closing disparities in health care in communities of color would be a priority. He has worked in a bipartisan manner on efforts like campaign finance reform, ethics reform, and immigration reform. I reluctantly supported McCain-Feingold but I only committed to this modest campaign reform effort after holding out for a long time. I held out a long time because I was concerned about many things in the law. The emergence of 527s, which for the most part allowed for unregulated independent expenditures was one concern I had. I wanted Congress to pass a strong public financing bill because we must get big money out of politics, and the only way to do that is through public financing.

McCain concerns me as a candidate because I have not seen his active involvement with the Congressional Black Caucus, Hispanic Caucus, Asian Pacific American Caucus, or the Progressive Caucus. His election would be a major setback to the civil and human rights gains we have made over the years, and I worry for our country and the world if he becomes our next president.

We must look to the leaders of the future to help us resolve the many issues that threaten our country, and I felt strongly that during the 2008 presidential campaign the person who could best lead the country was Barack Obama. I formerly stated my endorsement of Sen. Barack Obama (D-IL) in a press release in which I stated that:

As I've watched Senator Obama campaign for the Presidency, I am convinced that here is a man who is a real agent of change; a man who can lead our nation in this young century in a new and positive direction. This century cries for social, environmental, diplomatic, global, and neighborhood solutions to the misery that confronts far too many people in our own country and around the globe. I know that a President Obama would find a prompt and effective way to end the occupation of Iraq and that he would strengthen U.S. diplomacy and international development as an instrument of national policy to prevent crises that lead to war and conflagration.

I know that a President Obama would place education, health care, poverty, economic security, criminal justice reform, climate change and all of the important domestic issues at the top of his agenda. And, I know that a President Obama would make eradication of HIV/AIDS at home and abroad a top priority. As Andrew Sullivan so eloquently wrote in an *Atlantic* article this December: "At a time when America's estrangement from the world risks tipping into dangerous imbalance, when a country at war with lethal enemies is also increasingly at war with itself, when humankind's spiritual yearnings veer between an excess of certainty and an inability to believe anything at all, and when sectarian and racial divides seem as intractable as ever, a [person] who is a bridge between these worlds may be indispensable." I believe that the indispensable person at this time and for the office of President of the United States is Senator Obama.

I am honored to endorse Senator Obama's candidacy and will endeavor with all of my political commitment to help him secure the Democratic nomination for that highest office. This is a matter of conscience in a time that demands that we all follow our deepest beliefs. I share Senator Obama's vision and active commitment to building a society based on activism, progressive values and a keen sense that we must act now and outside of the usual bounds of partisanship and expediency.

Whatever the outcome of the 2008 presidential election, when the new administration comes to power in 2009, I intend to work very closely with the new president and cabinet on my agenda and on the agenda for my constituents and the organizations I represent. For example, I want the new president to put more resources into our domestic and global HIV/AIDS efforts. I want the new president to support legislation to cut poverty in half in the next decade. I would like the new president to normalize relations with Cuba. I would like to help reform our criminal justice system so that we can keep young boys out of jail and in school. I also intend to work on re-entry strategies, housing, and new approaches to public education as well as universal health care. As a member of the Appropriations Committee, I hope to work with a new White House on a budget that understands the value of increasing appropriations for education; green jobs; health care; historically black colleges and institutions that serve Hispanics and Native Americans; and programs like Upward Bound, Gear Up, and Trio, that help low- income students stay in school and go to college. Also a new administration will hear from me about major efforts in my district such as support for the Port of Oakland, a major economic engine in my district as well as many of the exciting and innovative projects that are unique to the Ninth Congressional District. And I will work with my colleagues to convince the new president that earmarks are a good thing and should be supported as long as they are transparent and aboveboard. Congressional districts such as mine need small amounts of federal funds for public entities and nonprofits to bring some equity and a decent quality of life to local residents. Perhaps wealthier districts don't need earmarks. Mine does. I will make this argument to the next president loud and clear.

Chapter Nine

> True heroism is remarkably sober, very undramatic. It is not the urge to surpass all others at whatever cost, but the urge to serve others at whatever cost.
>
> —Arthur Ashe

The morning of September 11th, I was on the Hill for an early morning meeting with the administrator of the Small Business Administration. I was concerned that because the Republicans had gained control of both the executive and legislative branches, federal assistance for women and minorities had been slashed, and as a former business owner I knew how devastating this could be. To find out what the status of programs for women and minorities was, some of the members of the Congressional Black Caucus, including myself, Reps. Diane Watson (D-CA), Sheila Jackson Lee (D-TX), and a few others, got up early to attend a breakfast meeting in one of the private dining rooms in the Capitol.

As usual, my agenda for the day kept changing, so I stepped out of the dining room around 8:45 a.m. to call my office and confirm my schedule. Danielle LeClaire, my Legislative Director, sounded very upset and told me an airplane had crashed into the World Trade Center in New York City. No one knew why and she asked if I wanted her to take me home. Obviously, it was terrible news but the magnitude of what she told me just didn't register. I didn't think it would have any significant effect on my day. I started walking back to the dining room when I heard a lot of people screaming "Evacuate the building!" Tom McDaniels, my administrative assistant, was with me, and we asked several people what was going on and which way we should run, but no one knew anything.

I took off my shoes and ran with Tom to the nearest exit. He reminded me there were reporters all around, cameras were taping, and I was running in my stocking feet. I didn't care, especially when I looked behind me and saw smoke in the distance, which I later learned was the result of American Airlines Flight 77 crashing into the Pentagon. I ran up Pennsylvania Avenue until I encountered Rep. Dennis Moore (D-KS), who was just returning from the dry cleaners and was carrying his clothes home. Dennis suggested I come to his house which was nearby. I reluctantly agreed because he lives on Capitol Hill, and I figured because whatever was happening had to do with the Capitol, his house was mighty close to any potential danger.

Dennis' wife Stephanie and his office staff were also at his house, and we watched in stunned silence as the attacks and their aftermath unfolded on television. I was unable to reach my family or staff by phone for quite a while because most of the phone lines were either down or overextended. Finally I was able to speak with a friend in San Francisco who I asked to call my family to let them know that I was fine. Then, we heard a report of another plane crash, this time in Pennsylvania. We now know United Airlines Flight 93 was headed to either the White House or the Capitol, and this is why we were evacuated.

I felt angry and worried. That evening almost every member of Congress went to a briefing at a temporary command center.

Later, we went to the Capitol because some of my fellow members felt the country should see us working and taking care of business—but when we got there we were advised not to go into the building. Instead, we congregated on the steps and sang "God Bless America." Everyone strongly believed in demonstrating to the public we were united as a country and prepared to deal with the attack. The whole situation was so confusing, and no one had any answers, but there was already speculation that al-Qaeda was behind these attacks.

During the next two days, our congressional briefings regarding these acts of terrorism were superficial. Profound anger, sorrow, and shock permeated the Hill and the country. I voted for several bills that denounced these attacks and provided emotional and financial support to the victims. One condemned the terrorist attacks, extended condolences to victims and their families, commended rescue workers, supported the determination of the President—in close consultation with Congress—to find justice for the victims and to punish the perpetrators and sponsors of these attacks. We decreed September 12 a national day of unity and mourning and a second decree expressed the sense of the U.S. Congress that Americans should fly the American flag. A third sped the payment of benefits to families of public safety officers killed or injured in the attacks, and a fourth provided tax relief to the victims of the attacks. We also provided $40 billion in emergency funding for increased public safety, antiterrorism activities, disaster recovery efforts, and assistance for the victims of the tragedy.

President Bush consulted with congressional leaders on what the appropriate response to these attacks should be. These discussions led to the concept of a joint congressional resolution authorizing the President to take military steps to deal with the responsible parties. We had several Democratic Caucus meetings to discuss our options for response and which resolutions would be most effective. We agreed that it was important to continue to emphasize to the country that we were united and nonpartisan. In these meetings, I voiced my concerns regarding our responsibilities as members of Congress and questioned whether some of the resolutions we were considering would be ceding too much power to the President. I argued Congress must both ensure and insist that our system of checks and balances remain intact and that whatever our response, we needed to be careful that it did not lead to more violence and death. Violence begets violence. I stressed that we should use this unfortunate historical opportunity to urge the use of restraint and develop an appropriate response that brought the terrorists to justice and dealt with terrorism in a real way, not start a war while our country, including its leadership, was still grieving and in shock. Several other members of the caucus voiced the same concerns.

Our Founding Fathers had grave reservations about giving the president too much power, which is why they specifically reserved the right to declare war to Congress alone, although the Constitution also gives the president the power to repel any attack on U.S. territory. This separation of powers was, overall, rigidly observed (the Civil War being a notable exception) until 1964 when the lines of authority between Congress and the president began to blur. That year, acting on reports that North Vietnamese boats had attacked two American destroyers off the coast of Vietnam, Congress, in a vote of 414–0 in the House and 88–2 in the Senate, approved the Gulf of Tonkin Resolution, authorizing President Lyndon Johnson to "take all necessary measures to repel an armed attack against the forces of the United States and to prevent further aggression." Johnson, in turn, used the powers granted to him in this resolution as a "blank check" to escalate the Vietnam War.

Several years later, as the war became increasingly unpopular and evidence of the alleged attack proved to be inaccurate, Congress passed the War Powers Resolution in 1973 which limits the president's powers to introduce American armed forces into actual or imminent hostility. Congress again took action to limit presidential authority in 1982 when the Senate learned that under the Reagan administration, the CIA had been funding Contra rebels in Nicaragua without its knowledge or consent.

But nothing had ever been as sweeping or so directly threatened the very fabric of our system of checks and balances as the resolution the Republicans sent us to review on September 13, 2001. One resolution stated:

> The President is authorized to use all necessary and appropriate force against those nations, organizations, or persons he determines planned, authorized, committed or aided the terrorist attacks that occurred on September 11, 2001, or harbored such organizations or persons, in order to prevent any future acts of international terrorism against the United States by such nations, organizations or persons.

Unlike all other major legislation authorizing the use of military force by the president, this joint resolution authorized military force against "organizations and persons" linked to the September 11, 2001 attacks. This authorization of military action against "organizations or persons" is unprecedented in American history. I was also troubled because it did not obligate the President to report back to Congress on any actions he would take over a 60-day period as had been required during the Gulf War.

Many agreed it was too broad and thus the late Reps. Tom Lantos (D-CA) and Ike Skelton (D-MO), ranking Democratic members of the House International Affairs Committee and House Armed Services Committee, sent the resolution back to the leadership and staff who drafted it, but in the end nothing much changed. I couldn't believe the Democrats wanted to give such broad powers to President George W. Bush to start a war, but that's what it boiled down to. The similarities between the Gulf of

Tonkin Resolution and this resolution, which Congress wanted to quickly approve, terrified and concerned me deeply. The Senate sent this resolution to the House to debate and vote on, on September 14th, a day earlier than anticipated. In addition to its expansion of the President's powers, it also bypassed the usual committee process, and there were no hearings held about it. It was only discussed by the Democratic and Republican caucuses and brought to the floor. I was alarmed at the rush to push this resolution through, as well as its ramifications. In fact, that morning, former Rep. Eva Clayton (D-NC) read the look on my face and said she knew how difficult this vote must be for me.

I decided not to attend the noon memorial service, which was being held at the National Cathedral so I could continue to talk to my staff and consider how I would vote on this. I went into the cloakroom, an informal place for members of Congress to congregate that is off-limits to the press. I spoke with Rep. Elijah Cummins (D-MD). He, too, was disturbed about the haste to rush to judgment. We discussed our reasons for not attending the memorial, and we both felt we just had too much to deal with at the time. In addition to keeping in touch with my district back in Northern California, my Chief of Staff, Sandré Swanson, was mourning the death of his cousin, Wanda Green. She was one of the nation's first African American flight attendants, and she died aboard the hijacked United Airlines jet that crashed in Pennsylvania. These brave people who I will always remember and honor, could have possibly saved my life that fateful morning.

Buses to transport congressional members to the memorial were out in front of the Capitol, and I could see my colleagues somberly boarding them. I changed my mind about attending the service and decided I wanted to reflect on, and pray for, the families and victims of this tragedy, and also to pray for myself to find the strength and insight to do what was right. I felt a sudden need to ask God for guidance and also thought taking a break from the political discussions about the resolution would be helpful. I told Elijah, "I think I'll go." I ran out into the cold September rain while someone held an umbrella over my head. I'm pretty sure I was the last one on the last bus. President Bush along with former Presidents George H.W. Bush, Bill Clinton, Jimmy Carter, and Jerry Ford were at the service. Although the mood at the church was somber, there was a spirit of revenge and retaliation, as was evidenced in part by President Bush's comment, "Just three days removed from these events, Americans do not yet have the distance of history. But our responsibility to history is already clear: to answer these attacks and rid the world of evil."

When Rev. Nathan Baxter, the dean of National Cathedral, delivered the invocation his words had a profound effect on me. Before that prayer, I had felt both saddened by the tragedy that had befallen our country, and at the same time I was worried because I felt the path we as leaders were taking was not the right one. I had been trying to rationalize voting for this horrible resolution that had so much support from other members of Congress and American citizens. But I also felt in my heart it was wrong and totally against my personal, political, and religious beliefs and the political beliefs of my constituents. I also believed that by supporting it, our country could become even more at risk and terrible things could happen as a result. I can't remember exactly what Rev. Baxter's words were at the time, but I know his sentiments were something along the lines of: despite our grief, let us hope that that we may not, through our actions become the evil we deplore. At that moment, a sense of peace and calm came over me, and I knew then I would vote against the resolution and would simply have to prepare for the repercussions.

After the service, I returned to my offices at the Capitol and by then, some constituents had called or e-mailed stating their opposition to this resolution, which helped steady my resolve. I talked to several friends, including my pastor, but this brief moment of peace was interrupted when my staff told me to get to the floor right away because the vote was coming up. I went into the Red Room, an office space for members of Congress just off the House floor, and called former Rep. Ron Dellums (D-CA). He told me he knew what I was going through, but made no effort to sway me either way. He walked me through the implications of what Congress was doing. We needed to show leadership and provide direction while the country was fearful and in mourning. He also pointed out that although we should condemn terrorism and bring to justice those who perpetrated the madness, going to war could allow violence to spiral out of control. Rep. Cynthia McKinney (D-GA) was in the Red Room, too, and she also spoke to Ron. After she hung up, she said, "I wish you could give me some of your constituents" as her way of acknowledging my district was more liberal than hers.

The tone of the five-hour debate that ensued was mixed. House Speaker Dennis Hastert (R-IL) opened it by saying, "We do this because we must preserve freedom and democracy in this country." Rep. Jerrold Nadler (D-NY), whose district included the World Trade Center Towers moved us when he said, "The charred rubble and thousands of dead Americans lying just blocks from my office in Manhattan, and hundreds more a stone's throw from this very building, demonstrate we have no choice. We must wage the war that has been thrust upon us." Some statements were far more hawkish like those made by Rep. Charlie Norwood (R-GA) who cautioned the terrorists, "We're coming after you, and the fury of hell is coming with us." Other statements more closely reflected my views, such as Rep. Lynn Woolsey (D-CA) who said although she would reluctantly support the resolution, she feared that, "Hasty action could mean killing even more innocent people." I quickly wrote a statement incorporating some of the words Marcus Raskin, a close friend and founder of the Institute for Policy Studies, provided me. When it was my turn to have the floor, I could barely speak. I was teary and feeling awful. But this is what I said:

> Mr. Speaker, I rise today with a heavy heart, one that is filled with sorrow for the families and loved ones who were killed and injured in New York, Virginia, and Pennsylvania. Only the most foolish or the most callous would not understand the grief that has gripped the American people and millions around the world. This unspeakable attack on the United States has forced me to rely on my moral compass, my conscience, and my God for direction. September 11 changed the world. Our deepest fears now haunt us. Yet I am convinced that military action will not prevent further acts of international terrorism against the United States. I know that this use-of-force resolution will pass although we all know that the president can wage war even without this resolution. However difficult this vote may be, some of us must urge the use of restraint. There must be some of us who say, "Let's step back for a moment and think through the implications of our actions today, let us more fully understand their consequences."
>
> We are not dealing with a conventional war. We cannot respond in a conventional manner. I do not want to see this spiral out of control. This crisis involves issues of national security, foreign policy, public safety, intelligence gathering, economics, and murder. Our response must be equally multifaceted. We must not rush to judgment. Far too many innocent people have already died. Our country is in mourning. If we rush to launch a counterattack, we run too great a risk that women, children, and other non-combatants will be caught in the crossfire. Nor can we let our justified anger over these outrageous acts by vicious murderers inflame prejudice against all Arab Americans, Muslims, Southeast Asians, and any other people because of their race, religion, or ethnicity. Finally, we must be careful not to embark on an open-ended war with neither an exit strategy nor a focused target. We cannot repeat past mistakes. In 1964, Congress gave President Lyndon Johnson the power

to "take all necessary measures" to repel attacks and prevent further aggression. In so doing, this House abandoned its own constitutional responsibilities and launched our country into years of undeclared war in Vietnam.

At that time, Senator Wayne Morse, one of two lonely votes against the Tonkin Gulf Resolution, declared, "I believe that history will record that we have made a grave mistake in subverting and circumventing the Constitution of the United States. I believe that within the next century, future generations will look with dismay and great disappointment upon a Congress which is now about to make such a historic mistake." Senator Morse was correct, and I fear we make the same mistake today. And I fear the consequences. I have agonized over this vote. But I came to grips with it in the very painful yet beautiful memorial service today at the National Cathedral. As a member of the clergy so eloquently said, "As we act, let us not become the evil that we deplore."

Afterward Reps. Steny Hoyer (D-MD) and Tom Lantos (D-CA) comforted me with hugs and said how courageous I was. I will never forget that. Then, it was the moment of truth. The bells rang, votes were cast, and the board was full of green lights. There was only one red one. I had no idea I would be the only one. Yikes. I didn't know it at the time, but it would later prove ironic that I would intone Sen. Morse's (D-OR) important historical stand against the war, because just one year later, a nonprofit organization founded in his name would honor me with their bi-annual 2002 Wayne Morse Integrity in Politics Award. This award is presented to an elected official who, like the late Sen. Morse (D-OR), demonstrates integrity and independence in politics, even at great political cost. I was nominated for my opposition to the expansion of presidential powers and the use of military power to launch pre-emptive strikes. It felt wonderful to have my mother with me when I went to Eugene, Oregon, to receive the award. I am so glad that she was able to witness this glorious moment. Although this was not the first time I had voted in opposition to war, it was the first time that I had been singled out and recognized for my willingness to go it alone. In 1999, I cast the sole dissenting vote against the Clinton administration's plans to bomb Yugoslavia over the conflict in Kosovo and said at the time, "It is completely impermissible for the President to commit troops to war, a right given only to the Congress by the Constitution." And in 1998, mine was one of only five votes that opposed renewed bombing in Iraq over its refusal to allow weapons inspections by the United Nations.

I went into the cloakroom and Reps. John Lewis (D-GA), Nancy Pelosi (D-CA), Corrine Brown (D-FL), and Stephanie Tubbs Jones (D-OH) all tried to get me to change my vote. They made comments like, "You can put a statement on record why you're opposed," "You are doing such good work on HIV/AIDS—we need you here and you could lose your election," and "We've got to be unified—even the peace community is silent." They were genuinely concerned about me as a friend. A few days later I ran into the late Cong. Henry Hyde (R-IL) who chaired the International Relations Committee on which I served. He looked stealthily around as if he didn't want anyone to see or hear him, leaned over and whispered to me that although he disagreed with my vote, he respected me for sticking to my convictions, and he mentioned that some of his Republican colleagues had discussed doing something similar. Although diametrically opposed to Chairman Hyde (R-IL) on many issues, especially his anti-choice position, just like the late Chairman Tom Lantos (D-CA), both white-haired white gentlemen, I grew to respect them and really liked them as human beings. Because of our mutual respect, I was able to get several bills passed and signed into law by President Bush. I miss them very much.

I was in such a lonely place—yet everyone who tried to get me to change my vote displayed sincere concern and friendship. After the vote I thought about how much my life had changed in the past few days. I had no idea how much more change was to come. When I returned to my office, the phones were ringing off the hook. The first call I took was from Jean Dickerson, the mother of my daughter-in-law Angie, who told me I was right and to hang in there. CNN left repeated messages asking for a statement or an interview. Angry calls flooded in too, which was particularly difficult for Sandré Swanson, who was in the awful position of taking many of these calls while still grieving for his cousin. As the calls and e-mails kept coming, a friend contacted Sandré and they talked about arranging security for me, which I opposed. But when I returned home, I checked my voice mail, and one of the messages sounded like someone was firing gunshots into the telephone. Capitol Hill Police came to my house and decided I needed protection. Other death threats came in as well.

What a nightmare it all was. For weeks, Capitol Hill Police officers sat in a car in front of my house, waited at my office, went to church with me, took me to the grocery store, and even accompanied me to Macy's. They traveled to and from California with me and coordinated with the Oakland Police department and the FBI. At that time, I was living at my former house while I was constructing a new one. They even accompanied me on site visits. I will always remember and thank them for their sense of professionalism and understanding. It wasn't until much later I learned the same problems were still with us. Angry phone calls, e-mails, and letters to local newspapers kept coming for weeks. All of the rage surrounding September 11th from misguided folk was directed at me. It was mainly the Right-wing. I was branded "a clueless liberal," chastised for my "complete utter lack of morality." My vote was called a "singular embarrassment to the citizens of the Ninth District of California." And in a column called "The Enemy Within," David Horowitz called me "an anti-American communist who supports America's enemies and has actively collaborated with them in their war against America."[1]

I have stood for democracy and the right for Americans to say what they believe without fear of retribution but the darker side of our country's attitudes to the war came as quite a shock to me. One of the more notable messages I received during that time was from a staunch ally, former Green Party member and California State Assemblywoman Audie Bock, who said she agreed with my vote. But just a few short weeks after this supportive message, Audie Bock criticized me for my stand and even went so far as to run against me in the March Democratic primary. She geared up a patriotic-themed campaign called "It's OK to Love America." The charges she leveled during her short-lived campaign were hurtful and slanderous. She claimed I was trying to "stick it" to the President while the country was still in mourning and on her website she accused me of "cowering behind bodyguards, knowing she has wronged both the living and the dead." She even put up a picture of me smiling with the World Trade Center burning in the background. I was, to say the least, flabbergasted; not only had I known Audie for years, but she was one of the hundreds of people who had left me a message acknowledging the courage I must have had to stand alone. I felt personally attacked, and my constituents thought this was pushing the limit on negative campaigning and reacted with a furor. What Audie and others forgot was that I had been in peril on that fateful September day because, by virtue of being a member of Congress in the Capitol building, I was one of hundreds of other public targets.

I was not the only public figure who suffered repercussions for responding to the tragic events of September 11 in a way that was different than the mainstream reaction. Host of the television show *Politically Incorrect*, Bill Maher was publicly rebuked by White House Press Secretary Ari Fleischer for saying during a broadcast, "We have been the cowards lobbing cruise missiles from 2,000 miles away. That's cowardly. Staying in the airplane when it hits the building, say what you want about it, it's not cowardly." Fleischer later responded that "Americans need to watch what they say, watch what they do, and this is not a time for remarks like that; there never is." Some of Maher's sponsors, including Federal Express and Sears, pulled their advertising, and the show was taken off the air in June 2002.

In the following months, I received more than 60,000 letters and e-mails, and I can't even begin to count how many phone calls I received. Approximately 60 percent of these messages were supportive. Bishop Desmond Tutu, as well as other world leaders and celebrities conveyed their support. Many people sent campaign contributions and so many flowers to my office it started to remind me of a funeral parlor after a while. Claire Greensfelder, another longtime friend, and until recently, the Executive Director of the Martin Luther King, Jr., Freedom Center, which I co-founded, kept message diaries for me. Numerous requests for speaking engagements and interviews came in.

My staff was initially divided on how to handle media requests, and some members of my staff felt it was important for me to clarify my reasons for casting this lone dissenting vote. I felt it was disrespectful to the dead and their surviving family members to engage in a national debate about my vote. Bodies were still being found. People were desperately grieving and angry. And as Gail Kaufman, my campaign manager and a longtime friend pointed out, I didn't need any more mess. I declined all but one national media request and did only a few interviews with the local press in California. In an interview I did with the *Los Angeles Times* toward the end of September, Marc Cooper asked me:

In the days following the vote, you were discussed widely on talk radio. People called you a traitor. They called you un-American and an accomplice of the terrorists. How do your respond to charges like that?[2]

I responded

> It's very painful, because I feel I'm just the opposite. I am an American who has tried to protect our democracy, who has tried to protect our system of checks and balances. If I hadn't, in the moment of adversity, tried to make sure that our Constitution stayed in place that would have been an abdication of my responsibility as an American citizen and as a representative. Many people misinterpreted my vote. Many simply believe that when you disagree, you are a traitor. But I say, when you disagree, you are demonstrating the beauty of this democratic system. And that's the true American way. I want to bring the perpetrators to justice, and I want to see a peaceful world.

Diane Sawyer asked to interview me the day after my vote, but I declined. Larry King wanted me on his show. I confirmed, and then cancelled. One of his production staff was angry and told my staff no one cancels on King. Barbara Walters kept calling, and I finally spoke with her. It was a pleasant conversation, and she clearly wanted to interview me. I did appear on a September 26, 2001, episode of the *Oprah Winfrey Show* titled "What Really Matters Now." I was part of a panel of distinguished women discussing the future of the nation's children. Famed poet Maya Angelou was also a guest, as were Peggy Noonan, Madeleine Albright, Marianne Williamson, Eve Ensler, Gloria Steinem, Faye Wattleton, and Ellen Goodman. Oprah gave me an opportunity to submit a videotaped message so I could address a national audience and explain my vote and my concerns for our children's future.

On the show I recounted my epiphany during Rev. Nathan Baxter's eloquent words during the 9/11 memorial service. Although I wasn't comfortable speaking about myself, I knew my vote was something people were interested in hearing about. I was far happier discussing the idea that especially after September 11, what really matters is our children, whose causes I have long advocated. I told Oprah's audience, "As women we must insist that our response is instructive to our children on how they deal with violence and that our response reassures our children that they will inherit a peaceful world. Women must do that . . . who else can do that?"

There were people who went out of their way to show their love and support. A couple of days after the September 14th vote, my friend and colleague Rep. Maxine Waters (D-CA) invited me to dinner. This was when all hell was breaking loose, and I had heavy security. We met at a restaurant on Connecticut Avenue in Washington. She was reassuring and supportive and said others should have voted no and commended me for my courage. Also, the following weekend, friends like Reps. Eddie Bernice Johnson (D-TX) and Corrine Brown (D-FL), and her daughter, invited me to go shopping and have lunch with them. It seemed like everyone close to me knew how hard a place to be this was. But in spite of my fears and uncertainties, I felt resolved in my decision and at peace with myself. These great, smart, tough, kind, yet sensitive women, as well as many other men and women, in many ways helped me get through this period, and I can't thank them enough.

My friend Charles Stephenson and his wife, Judith, knew my anguish and with love and kindness reached out to me that Sunday. They invited me to go to church with them. Along with my security detail, we went to Union Temple Baptist Church, where the prayers, music, and sermon by a prophetic preacher and teacher, Rev. Dr. Michael Eric Dyson, helped settle my spirit. Based on the congregation's response to me, I realized that the black community understood this defining and tragic moment and my response to it.

In the days and weeks that followed that vote, there were several critical and defining moments. The first one was at a fund-raiser in late September for Rev. Jesse Jackson's Rainbow PUSH Coalition at the Four Seasons Hotel in Washington, DC, with Bill Cosby, who was the special guest. Bill's office called and said he really wanted me to come over to his hotel so he could meet me before the event. I reluctantly went with one of my security guards. We went up to his room, and he was delighted to meet me. He told me he and his wife Camille watched my speech live on C-SPAN and said it was perfect. He then called her, and I spoke with her as well—she was gracious and complimentary. We went downstairs for dinner. The guests were mostly corporate folks and, of course, Rev. Jesse Jackson was there as well. When Bill Cosby got up—oh boy— his accolades and praise for me led to a standing ovation in my honor. Even Jesse was on his feet. Rev. Jackson is one of the greatest civil and human rights leaders of our time whose candidacy for president paved the way for many of us to be elected to public office. Rev. Jackson asked me to speak at a Rainbow Coalition conference in Chicago a couple of years later where he presented me with a beautiful award. His support has been unwavering. Three or four weeks later, the progressive community organized a rally of more than 3,500 people in front of the Oakland City Hall in support of my commitment to peace. It was a bleak, cold day, but that was not what was preventing me from attending. In addition to the ongoing security concerns, I thought it would be better to let the community show its support without my presence. But as I listened to the rally on the radio, my instincts told me I should go for just a few minutes, to thank people for their support, and to make a short statement. I arrived two hours into the rally. Danny Glover was there, and he called me a "hero." Alice Walker was there too, and she said I was "inspiring."

It was unbelievable—the applause, the poems, the music. There were people holding signs that read "Barbara Lee for President" and "You go girl!" and "Barabara Lee Speaks For Me"—which students at Mills College coined. Danny and Alice escorted me to the podium, and I thanked the crowd for being great patriots and great

Americans. I also said something about supporting our troops, which this crowd didn't relate to, but I support the courage and sacrifices our troops make, and I felt it was important to mention that. I also hoped this statement would help to insulate me from attacks that were branding me unpatriotic. Reports about this rally ran in many newspapers, including *The New York Times*, and some members of Congress took note. People started saying things like, "At least there was one person saying something different." It gave others the space to say, "Yes, she's right," that just kept snowballing. People began in a quiet way, saying, "Maybe she is on to something." This kept a lot of potential criticism and attacks from credible sources quiet. Now my colleagues could feel better in supporting me because they could say, "her district supports her, look at all the people who turned out."

Another important moment came after the Congressional Black Caucus Dinner. Thousands of African Americans come to Washington, DC, every year for the annual legislative weekend sponsored by the Congressional Black Caucus Foundation. It is held at the Washington Convention Center with brain trusts and workshops on every policy issue important to the black community and to the entire country. Walking through the convention center that weekend with my security detail revealed how the black community interpreted my vote. They got it. Everywhere I went people thanked me, spoke words of inspiration, and told me they were praying for me.

Speaking of prayer, so many members of the clergy and the faith community got in touch with me and said they prayed for me at church. Believe it or not I could feel the awesome power of prayer in a way I had never felt before. To this day I run into people who told me they prayed and continue to pray for me. What an affirmation of the presence of God in my life this is.

A reception was held in my honor, and many people came, including Susan Taylor, former editor-in-chief of *Essence* magazine. Reps. Don Payne (D-NJ), Mel Watt (D-NC), Bobby Scott (D-VA), Maxine Waters (D-CA), and others said they should have voted with me. They gave public speeches, and surrounded me in a protective circle of love, concern, and humility. It was an awesome moment. In addition, Rep. John Conyers (D-MI) added a statement into the *Congressional Record*, which said in part:

> I rise to show my support for our colleague, Congresswoman Barbara Lee. I am concerned about recent reports that violent threats have been directed at Ms. Lee following her vote against H.J. Res. 64, which authorized the use of military force in response to the attacks of September 11. While many of us may not agree with Congresswoman Lee's decision to vote against the authorization of the use of force, we must stand united to defend her right to vote her conscience as a member of the United States House of Representatives. A member's duty is to vote on behalf of their constituents and to vote with their conscience. We must rise in support of this intrinsic component of our democracy.

He really came to my defense.

The aftermath of the September 11th attacks on our country affects our lives to this day. Bush used that horrible moment to not only topple the Taliban government that controlled Afghanistan at the time, but he also used the powers granted to him in the questionable resolution as the basis to use force to invade and occupy Iraq a year later. Antiwar marches and rallies began happening around the world. I participated in two of them in San Francisco and one in Oakland with Harry Belafonte. Some groups have used my September 14th speech to express their opposition to war. I'll never forget some children reciting my speech to me in the parking lot of the Allen Temple Baptist Church in Oakland where I regularly attend church when I am in my district.

There are many failures in our collective response to the events of September 11, 2001. We were wrong as a country to believe that we could forever be insulated from foreign attacks. I believe that in our haste to try to correct this mistake, we have made even greater mistakes that have ended the lives of thousands of brave American troops and cost our country billions of dollars. We are, as of this day, no closer to bringing Osama bin Laden to justice, and there is no foreseeable end to our involvement in Iraq and Afghanistan.

As for me, there are things I might have done differently, too. Maybe I should have kept my shoes on. Maybe I should have more fully realized how difficult it would be to stand alone in a sea of fear and complacency. Maybe I should have been less apprehensive about talking to the press and its potential repercussions. But the one thing I would not do differently is change my vote on this resolution despite the personal ramifications I endured for a while. I am proud I used my moral compass and my ear for the voices of my constituents and people throughout the world to be a lone voice of reason at one of our nation's most trying times. This has been the most humbling moment of my life.

Notes

1. David Horowitz, "Horowitz's Notepad: An Enemy Within," *Front-PageMagazine.com*, September 19, 2001. http://www.frontpagemag.com/Articles/Read.aspx?GUID=6BCF9E6A-6C55-411A-9DD8-145E97FD8740.

2. Marc Cooper, "Rep. Barbara Lee: Rowing Against the Tide," *Los Angeles Times*, September 23, 2001. http://mailman.lbo-talk.org/2001/2001-September/019268.html.

Chapter Ten

For in the end, freedom is a personal and lonely battle; and one faces down fears of today so that those of tomorrow might be engaged.

—Alice Walker

When I look back over my life, I see trailing behind me a winding road that at various points has been broken up by fits and starts. Some paths seem to have veered off in divergent directions, which then came to an abrupt halt and then pick up an entirely new path. I may not have known where I was headed, but each step has been guided by my faith. It's to God that I turn for solace in moments of uncertainty. My faith in God has sustained me in even my darkest hours and when I feel challenged, I dig my heels in deep and do not budge until I see a cause or project through to its conclusion.

After my lone vote, my mother said, "They should have asked me why you wouldn't change your vote regardless of the repercussions. I could have told them to forget it." Those who know me well are familiar with my stand on many issues and know that I have often been considered the "darling of the liberals." Good! I want people to know that my convictions are not for sale to the highest bidder and that I vote with my heart and my head—even if it means becoming a pariah, the butt of jokes, or a target for malicious fear mongers. I'm not blind or insulated. I strive to keep in touch with the values and desires of my constituents by spending countless hours in my congressional district meetings with the residents to help improve their lives in whatever way I can. I keep the people in my district up-to-date on what I am doing on their behalf. I make sure that they know who I am, that I am accountable, and that they have access to my office if they need to reach me. My Washington, DC and district office staff members are phenomenal and work 24-7 on behalf of my constituents and my legislative agenda. My advisors, volunteers, and Team Lee give countless hours supporting my efforts. I owe them all a debt of gratitude.

The people throughout my district have always known how I stand on a range of issues. When I was in the California Assembly, the "three strikes" law was passed. I actively opposed it in the state legislature. I was one of only a scant few members voting against it, and for that opposition, I received numerous death threats. Right-wing talk radio hosts crucified me. Once again, I felt in a very personal way, this is the price one pays for bucking what is popular. It was a horrible time. Later in the California Senate, I introduced legislation to modify the law to require that the "third strike" be a violent offense to qualify for the 25-to-life sentence. Most of the major newspapers in California supported this bill. Unfortunately, it was one of the few bills that I could not get off the floor during my tenure in the California Legislature. I believe thirteen members of the senate voted for it, and I needed 21 to get it to the governor's desk. Unfortunately, Democrats helped to defeat this. And even more unfortunate is that exactly what I predicted has come true. Our prison population is soaring with primarily African American and Latino men. Our prison budget in California provides for a "prison industrial complex," and billions of dollars are being wasted.

It's a sad commentary about how far we have yet to go when in my own state of California, there has only been one new college opened since 1984, but there have been twenty-one new prisons opened. That's why, since my days in the California state legislature, I have been committed to reforming the way our criminal justice system works. While still in the state legislature, I established the California Commission on the Status of African American Males and led the fight to restore rehabilitation to the mission of the state prison system. Since coming to Congress, I have continued to fight for prison and criminal justice reforms, and I am a member of the Public Safety, Sentencing, and Incarceration Reform Caucus. I worked on a comprehensive, bipartisan plan to reform ex-prisoner re-entry programs, to reinstate the right to vote for ex-offenders, and to provide for federal record expungement. I continue to work with community organizations and the court system to change the way ex-offenders are transitioned back into society, to help them clear up their criminal records. In Oakland in 2004, along with the Congressional Black Caucus Foundation, I hosted a conference on the Status of the African American Male.

As a former member of the House International Relations Committee who was also the most senior Democratic female member, and now as a member of the Foreign Operations sub-committee of the Appropriations Committee and also the Foreign Affairs Committee, I have seen what difference diplomacy can make in resolving conflict and avoiding violence. When Congress was debating the authorization for the use of force against Iraq, I introduced a substitute measure to ensure that inspections and diplomatic options were exhausted before taking any military action. My intent was to prevent us from going to war without a time for reflection or without any sort of serious consideration of the consequences, which is why I authored legislation to disavow the Bush adminis-tration's doctrine of pre-emption. The very concept of preemption is anathema to our moral code as a nation. How can we in good conscience engage in an unprovoked attack against another nation and then criticize others who engage in the same tactics? We don't have to look far to see how wrong pre-emptive action is and how destructive it can be to global peace and stability. Of course, the president always has the authority to use military force to attack in case of an imminent threat.

I travel abroad to help heighten awareness of sovereign nations and their overall development process, examining such issues as what the United States should support and what countries need, women's education and health, famine and food security, and HIV/AIDS. What a privilege it has been meeting with heads of state such as President Ellen Johnson Sirleaf, of Liberia, who is the first female head of state in Africa—and a brilliant woman. I try to develop better exchanges in communication between the United States and other countries and with individuals, organizations, and cities in my congressional district. For example, I have been work-ing with City of Oakland officials, the Oakland Zoo, and Chinese officials to help bring pandas to the zoo, which would be a major economic and tourist boon. I have traveled with businesses in my district to help develop better trade and business ties with other countries. On many occasions I have taken people to Cuba to edu-cate them about the realities of Cuban society so that they can make judgments for themselves whether the negative propaganda about Cuba that we consume in the United States is justified. I have met with former President Fidel Castro on numerous occa-sions. I also have traveled to the Darfur region in the Sudan three times and Chad once, to witness firsthand the horrific genocide taking place. I did this so I could find out for myself what I needed to do to help bring an end to the genocide. The first time I went to

Darfur was as part of a congressional delegation that included Academy Award-nominated actor Don Cheadle, star of the phenomenal movie *Hotel Rwanda*. *Nightline* documented the journey and later aired a broader segment on the conditions in Darfur so that Americans could better understand that genocide was occurring on our watch.

I think that it is morally repugnant for the international community to be so reluctant to describe conditions in Rwanda and Darfur as genocide. The scale of violence in Rwanda in the early 1990s was unimaginable and swift, and I often say that we should never again sit silent and watch another genocide take place. In Rwanda, nearly 1 million people were killed in just a few months, and all our country could do was "apologize" as President Bill Clinton did years later. To address the genocide that occurred in Rwanda and Darfur, over the years I have met with the President of Algeria, Abdelaziz Bouteflika and Egypt's President Mohammed Hosni Mubarak several times along with several colleagues. I have met with ambassadors from Arab nations as well as China. I asked each for help in order to gain some leverage and bring an end to the genocide. They acknowledged that terrible things had happened or were happening but got very uncomfortable when pressed to call it what it was. While in Sudan, I witnessed the suffering of people who were the victims of atrocities committed by the Janjaweed. These state-sponsored murderers were brought in by the government to preempt any attempt on the part of the people or rebels to establish autonomy. I have seen refugees displaced by the genocide in Darfur struggle to survive in a land burdened by ethnic and tribal hatred, drought, desertification, and untold deaths.

When we spoke about Darfur, our nation and others offered lots of excuses and talked about what we were doing on the humanitarian front. That's great, but it was not the real deal; we should have used our leverage with Khartoum to pressure the government to end the suffering. I have pushed for divestment of state pension funds like CalPERS, and for colleges, universities, and public entities to divest their portfolios of stocks of companies that do business in the Sudan. I believe we must hit Sudan in its pocketbook, as we did with the apartheid regime in South Africa. President Bush reluctantly signed my divestment legislation in December 2007 but issued a statement signaling that he really wanted the option to get around this law. I was furious. He signed the bill because he knew that Congress would override his veto. This was a unanimous vote. Again this is an example of how Bush says one thing—condemns genocide—yet he won't take strong actions to stop it.

On behalf of my work on the HIV/AIDS pandemic, I traveled to Durban, South Africa; Barcelona, Spain; Bangkok, Thailand; and Toronto, Canada, to attend the International AIDS Conference. At the Toronto conference I decided that we should try to remove the travel ban prohibiting those living with HIV/AIDS from coming into the United States. This travel ban is a terrible human rights violation, and I want the United States to host an International AIDS Conference to improve awareness of the problems. American citizens should benefit from information, interaction, and solidarity with the rest of the world in fighting this pandemic. So, in August 2007, I introduced legislation to repeal this ban. I worked with Sen. John Kerry (D-MA), and he picked this issue up in December 2007. We successfully worked together and were able to get the repeal of the ban into the March 2008 HIV/AIDS Reauthorization Bill. I am proud of our efforts because this had been just "a brainstorm" I had in Toronto. I worked hard to get this done.

There is no doubt that Bush has helped focus more resources and attention to fighting HIV/AIDS on an international level. I will never forget the first meeting the Congressional Black Caucus held with him right after he was elected. I wore a beaded pin with a red ribbon made by women in South Africa to raise funds for HIV/AIDS programs. He admired this pin, and I told him why I was wearing it. I took the opportunity to tell him that he needed to focus attention on this pandemic. He agreed and said he wanted to work with me to do something about it. I was pleased that he mentioned fighting HIV/AIDS in his first State of the Union speech, but it was an uphill battle about the amount of money we should have invested in the effort, the ideological battles over "abstinence-only" policies, and the use of condoms in our efforts to stop the spread of the disease, support for local efforts, and many more difficult hurdles.

For my work to end genocide, stamp out HIV/AIDS, and address injustice—including my fight to get Congress to investigate the CIA, NSA, and U.S. military's role in the coup d'état that removed the democratically elected president, Haitian Pres. Jean Bertrand Aristide—in 2005 I was nominated for the Nobel Peace Prize as part of the project initiated in 2003 called 1000 Women for the Nobel Peace Prize. Only 12 women have received the Nobel Peace Prize since it was first awarded in 1901, and according to organizers, the 1000 Women Project was developed to find 1,000 exemplary women to collectively receive this rare and prestigious prize. These influential and tireless heroes represented millions of nameless women worldwide who have changed the world and worked for justice, education, political rights, and security. The nominees from more than 150 countries were a diverse cross-section of women: farmers, teachers, activists, artists, and politicians, and I was honored and humbled to be counted among them.

Whether it's women struggling to stem the tide of soil degradation, desertification, or developing alternative fuel sources, women and men must seek solutions to the diminishing supplies of fossil fuels, increasing pollution, and the impact of global warming if we are to turn a healthy planet over to future generations. Scientists say that unless we curb global warming emissions, average U.S. temperatures could be three to nine degrees higher by the end of the century. Though the United States makes up just 4 percent of the world's population, it produces 25 percent of the carbon dioxide pollution from fossil fuels—by far the largest share of any country. In fact, the United States emits more carbon dioxide than China, India, and Japan combined. Oakland is a city that prides itself on its forward "green" attitudes toward construction, pollution, energy consumption, and carbon dioxide emissions. I have tried to reflect the wishes of the people in my district and have advocated in Congress that we must address the issue of climate change, work to reduce emissions, increase energy efficiency, adopt the Kyoto Protocol, and fund research on safe, clean, affordable energy resources that were slashed from the Environmental Protection Agency's (EPA) budget.

I hope to show by example that in spite of the obstacles that we encounter in life, people, particularly women and people of color, can do something with their lives that is meaningful. Women and people of color can break glass ceilings; each of us must use our experiences, good or bad, to change our communities, our country, and the world. But to do this, we must not feel like or be a victim of past circumstances. We must each work hard to overcome low self-esteem, the effects of abuse, insecurity, poverty, violence, and injustice. We can't get bitter or angry because those emotions prevent us from moving forward. We must take on these challenges regardless of childhood indiscretions, domestic violence, confusion, anger, discrimination, and injustice. One person *can* make a difference. But it's not easy. To change society, individuals must change themselves, become who they are, and know themselves. Personal growth is never an easy road to travel. For African Americans, and for me, this was never as evident as when I made my first trip to the West Indies in 1973. After I graduated from Mills College, I treated myself to a cruise with my dear friend, the late Mary Burns and her two daughters. We flew to Florida and then traveled to St. Thomas, the Virgin Islands, the Dominican Republic, and Haiti. When we arrived I was truly surprised to discover black people were the racial majority in Haiti and St. Thomas and that like my ancestors and the ancestors of other African Americans, they too had been brought from Africa as victims of the gruesome slave trade. But what really saddened me the most was the abject poverty in which so many of them lived. Seeing so many people living in squalid conditions made me sad and angry. But the beautiful beaches, art, culture, food, Caribbean music and most of all, the spirit of the people, were wonderful. I felt at home in this tropical paradise and continue to daydream about someday living on a Caribbean island because I love the people of this region and their African spirit.

After this life-changing trip, I was determined to find a way to help with development in Caribbean and African countries. I have since taken trade, cultural, and educational delegations there. I helped convince the Cuban government to admit low-income African American and Latino students into the medical school in Cuba. I was national president of the U.S.–Grenada Friendship Society, and I worked on foreign policy issues involving the Caribbean when I was a staff member for Rep. Ron Dellums (D-CA). Following my first trip to the West Indies, this part of the world became the embodiment of what I imagined Africa would be like. I discovered people who were secure, independent, ran their own country, and lived free of the racism that I dealt with everyday. No matter which island I visited I felt liberated, which was a groundbreaking experience for a black person who lived in a majority white country. Just setting foot in countries where I was part of the majority population was empowering, and it made me feel that I could go with the flow, instead of going against the grain.

Of all my trips abroad, the most life altering and meaningful to me as an African American woman came in 1980 when I made my first trip to Africa. The whole trip came about when Rep. William Gray (D–PA) was leading a Congressional delegation to a conference sponsored by the African American Institute in Sierra Leone. Congressman Dellums couldn't go, so I went as his representative. Among the people who joined our delegation were Ambassador Andrew Young and Rep. Toby Moffit (D-CT). To reach Africa we traveled by military aircraft and during our flight were lucky to have been served a soul food meal on the plane. During the conference I remember meeting John F. Kennedy, Jr. who was there with his mother's companion, Maurice Tempelsman, who had a diamond business with interests on the continent. I will always remember John Jr. for his smiling face, beautiful hair, and handsome good looks.

During the trip, we also traveled to Nigeria, Senegal, and the Ivory Coast. As I visited each country, I noticed that the living conditions bore striking similarities to those in the Caribbean. I found that the living conditions were just as poor, that poverty was widespread. Yet despite the harsh conditions, there was much to admire, and I felt the same spirit and energy I had experienced in the Caribbean. I knew that my heart and soul were finally at peace. I finally felt that I had reached my homeland and this experience filled me with contentment and made me feel much more secure and relaxed as a black American. After traveling to Africa, I felt I could cope with being a black American living in the United States because I knew I had a motherland that is a continent of great beauty, filled ancient developed cultures, unique religions and people, and important natural resources. It was at this point that I at last felt I was closing the circle on my existence as a minority in America.

Years later in the early 1990s, I organized a California legislative delegation to Africa, and we visited Nigeria, Senegal, South Africa, Zimbabwe, Namibia, Côte d'Ivoire but also went to Ghana. I knew as soon as I stepped foot onto Ghanaian soil that I had reached the land of my family's ancestors. This touch with my past is an experience that the Ghanaians call "sankofa," and it's an experience that is very important for African Americans. Translated literally, sankofa means "it is not taboo to go back and fetch what you forgot." Visually and symbolically, sankofa is expressed as a mythic bird that flies forward while looking backward, with an egg symbolizing the future, clutched in its mouth. Sankofa is a principle that teaches us that we must go back to our roots to move forward. It tells us that we need to reach back and gather the best of what our past has to teach us and learn from our mistakes so that we can achieve our full potential as we move forward. Whatever we have lost or forgotten, whatever is forgone or stripped away, can be reclaimed, revived, preserved, and perpetuated.

As we met the people of Ghana during our visit, I was overcome by the warmth and feeling of kinship that they shared with me. Many of the people I met looked at me and told me I was a Fante, an ethnic group that are part of the Akan peoples of Ghana and the Ivory Coast. These people come from a long line of ancient tribes who have been renowned for their art for untold centuries, and they have a proud and rich heritage. They immediately responded to me because at just a glance they could see that many of my features resembled their own, and this connection to my lineage became very real for me with each passing day. This tie to the Fante was not just a coincidence though because I believe my ancestors on my biological father's side came from Ghana, and it made the experience that much more personal and revealing. Of all of my time in Ghana, one of the most exciting moments for me came when a Ghanaian village gave me the honor of becoming its queen mother. This is a special and highly regarded position because a queen mother is a chief who is responsible for helping the village. As part of my induction ceremony I wore a colorful traditional kente cloth wrapped around me in a graceful drape and was then hoisted onto a throne that was carried through the village. The kente cloth of the Ashanti people of Ghana is reserved for only the most important of ceremonies and has always been the cloth of kings. To wear it was a mark of high esteem, and I was truly honored to be a part of this important event. The celebration and parade through the village was not only a high point but was followed by a personally gratifying naming ceremony where I was presented with an African name "Nana Araba Mboraba," which means "born on Tuesday." This day has become one of my most fond memories not just of my trip but in my life, and it was a powerful affirmation that I am part of a never-ending line of strong and honorable people. My time in Ghana and my tribal connection to the Fante have given me a history that I can look back on with love and pride. I raise small sums of money for the children of Ghana and one of the projects is to help fund construction of five kindergartens. I was humbled and overwhelmed by the excitement of teachers, parents, and residents of the villages during the kick-off of this effort and the sparkle of hope in the children's eyes. Their thankfulness—demonstrated through song, dance, and poetry—was a life-affirming moment for me.

These enriching and rewarding voyages along with my early childhood experiences, my struggles to overcome challenges as a young woman raising two sons as a single mother, my education and training in social work, my faith in God, my work to bring about change, and my battles with discrimination, all have become part of the mosaic of who I am today. Just like the dazzling multicolored kente cloth woven from vibrant thread, each of us is a part of the fabric of humanity. What I have learned is that it is important for all of us to remember sankofa and be familiar with our roots so that each and every one of us can make a difference in the world. I am reminded of clichés I heard as child that are more powerful and relevant as I grow older: "pretty is as pretty does," "stop looking in the mirror, it's not what's outside your head but what's inside that matters," "what goes around comes around," "God looks out for fools and babies," "if you can't say something nice about someone, don't say anything at all," "God don't love ugly," "it's just a matter of time," and "every dog has his day." Each one of these old phrases may seem trite, but for me they send the message that if we are to understand the problems of the world and affect change, we must first look back at the paths that life has brought us down and know that although our routes may have been different along the way, that we are all part of an ongoing journey of discovery. If we are to find our way, we must look inward and improve who we are as individuals. We cannot change our communities, countries, and the global village if we aren't first ready to change ourselves. If we embrace our diversity and accept others for their uniqueness then we can come together in peace. God will be there to guide us, but only if we first recognize our strengths and use them to do His work.

Since 1990 I have literally lived in two places. First, while in the California Legislature from 1990 to 1998, I lived in Sacramento and Oakland, and since 1998 I have commuted from Washington, DC to Oakland nearly every weekend. This is the lifestyle of Members of Congress, and it is not glamorous or easy. But it is exciting, wonderful, and satisfying. My friends can't believe that in the midst of this constant work, flying back and forth from Washington, DC, to Oakland and around the world, I designed, built, and decorated a house—something I have wanted to do forever—with the help of a creative and brilliant woman, Altonia Anderson. I read all of the design and decorating magazines and have grown to love architecture and have an elementary knowledge of this profession. My favorite architects are Ricardo Legorreta, a wonderful, spiritual man who was a student of the world; renowned Luis Barragán; Frank Lloyd Wright whose "Fallingwater" house in Pennsylvania I have visited twice; and developer Joseph Eichler whose glass atrium-inspired houses that bring the outdoors inside, excite me. I would like to believe that my house is a combination of all three of their styles.

In the midst of such an intense life, I find comfort and peace in hanging out with my two sons Tony and Craig, their wives Angela and Memuna, and my four, soon-to-be five, grandchildren Jordan, Joshua, Jonah, and Simone. I don't get to spend as much girl time as I would like with my sisters Mildred and Beverly, my aunts Juanita and Lois, my cousin Zenobia and all of my cousins on the Lewis side of my family, and my girlfriends, and I would like more time to be with my mother Mildred, listening to music, watering my 40 plants, reading novels by African American men and women, and checking out arts and crafts, which I love to collect. One day, I will start playing the piano again. I still have the same piano that my grandfather bought me when I was three years old, and it's a shame that I can't find the time to practice. The real simple things in life bring me a sense of security, peace, and renew my spirit. If I had it to do over again, I would probably be a musician, artist, writer, or architect. But then again, only God has His way, and I would not be able to determine this. So, this is my story. This is my song. At the end of this road I hope I can say as it does in the Bible in 2 Timothy 4:7: "I have fought a good fight, I have finished (my) course, I have kept the faith."

$\propto$

Conclusion

As I write this afterword I am contemplating what's in store for me
as I continue my work to help build an America that can hold its
head high and once again be a part of the community of nations.
But I know that's not for me to know or decide. As a country, we
have been mocked, ignored, marginalized, feared, and ostracized by
many of our friends and allies for our reliance on violence to
achieve political and diplomatic goals, and we have been ridiculed
for our treatment of the poor. Our inability to work collaboratively
to end the HIV/AIDS pandemic and our insistence on forcing our
culture and values on reluctant countries have made us a pariah,
and we have been accused of hypocrisy. Poverty and peace are
linked, and if poverty is not eradicated, justice and peace are almost
impossible to achieve. In 2005, I wrote an article for the *Oakland
Tribune* that spoke about the way poverty has influenced us in ways
that are often considered to be the realm of Third World countries
where war, drought, disaster, and genocide lead to refugees fleeing
their homes in search of safety. In that article I stated that:

> The devastation wrought by hurricane Katrina has torn down the
> curtain and exposed the dirty secret that divides our nation like an

open wound. If anyone ever doubted that there were two Americas, hurricane Katrina and our government's shameful response to it have made the division clear for all to see. The brutal fact is that the majority of people who died in this tragedy were poor, primarily African Americans. Many were old and disabled. When the disaster came, people who had cash in the bank and a car in the garage escaped, and those who did not were shamefully left to fend for themselves.

The incompetence and indifference demonstrated by the administration in responding to this tragedy was shocking, but it wasn't surprising. Does anyone doubt that if this sort of devastation had taken place in the communities where the small percentage of people who are benefiting from the Bush administration's tax cuts live, the response would have been swift and efficient? This indifference to the most vulnerable among us is part and parcel of a systemic problem that seeks to make a large sector of our population invisible. Many people, viewing the human tragedy left in Katrina's wake, thought they were witnessing a tragedy in Somalia, Haiti or Sudan. Some even came to refer to the survivors as "refugees," as if the images were too foreign for them to recognize them as Americans. They thought, this does not look like the America that I know. For some of us, however, this is an America we know too well, an America that is too often swept under the rug by lawmakers and the media.

During the Bush presidency, the number of poor people in America grew by 17 percent. This is the real state of the so-called ownership society. And it is unacceptable. The problem with the Bush administration's response to Katrina was not simply the failure to react to the hurricane in a coherent or competent manner, it was the tragic failure to acknowledge the massive structural crisis that poverty and inequality pose for our nation and the stubborn refusal to conceive of any constructive role for our government in addressing it. I call on the American people to demonstrate that our nation is not indifferent to the least among us. We must make eradication of poverty a priority in this nation. America has been shocked by the images that have exposed this terrible divide in our nation. It is up to us now to decide whether our government has a responsibility to help improve the lives of the millions of Americans who are living in poverty or whether we will again abandon them to the dirty water to fend for themselves. I pledge that I will continue to sponsor legislation to bring an end to poverty and to create effective, long-term solutions that are part of an economic stimulus plan that strives to build a healthy economy that is not built on the backs of the workers. We are a nation with a strong economy and the largest concentration of wealth in the world. We can find inclusive, innovative ways to create jobs that offer people livable wages. We only have to change our priorities. Rather than spend more money on war, we can reinvest in the most valuable resource we have: our people.

As we know, if you are poor you cannot afford to eat well, live in a safe, clean environment, and you most definitely cannot afford to get sick. As part of an effort to raise awareness as to why we should increase the amount of food stamps provided to the poor, I participated in the "food stamp challenge" and lived off of $3.00 per day for one week, which was the average for food stamp recipients. I got a glimpse of why low-income people have higher rates of diseases such as high blood pressure and diabetes and shorter life spans. In my diary I noted that I would be off the diet in seven days but it haunted me that there were millions of people who were not so lucky.

If you are poor you will also be more likely to be a victim of violence. Violence has seeped into our culture and it permeates our lives in ways that have changed us as a people. We must address this predilection for violence because it has now become our solace of first, rather than last resort, and we are becoming a country where the military—not diplomacy—guides our foreign policy. I am part of a growing groundswell of people around the world who are no longer willing to accept the status quo of preying on people's fears, prejudices, and differences and using violence to resolve conflicts, whether it's among people or nations. The time is right to make a change and to create a vision for the future that is inclusive and relies on emphasizing what we have in common with others, rather than focusing on our differences. The worldwide peace movement is gaining momentum and is working for peace by encouraging the democratic principles of freedom, justice, and rule of law, and using nonviolent resistance and civil disobedience as tools to achieve positive goals. I am proud that my mother instilled in me the belief that civil rights for blacks, women, and all minorities are fundamentally human rights. She taught me that I have a duty to fight for better opportunities for all Americans and to be mindful of where I came from. I have seen this same activism in my sons as they have charted their own futures. My older son Tony continues to work on behalf of the uninsured and is a partner in Dickerson Employee Benefits, the largest African American-owned health insurance brokerage consulting firm in the United States. Tony is a gifted film writer, has casted several films, and has great sensitivity for conveying emotion with drama and pictures and words. Craig is a senior underwriter and business analyst at State Farm insurance company and brings his sense of stability, focus, and insight to his job. He is a very perceptive young black man who knows how to budget and save money. Both of my sons cook, clean house, take care of the children, and treat their wives like I believe a man should treat a woman. Their wives, Angela and Memuna, are beautiful, bright, superb mothers.

When I try to envision the future of our country, I see a nation where peace, and the conditions that are necessary for peace, are top priorities in America. For many years now I have worked with other peace activists to establish a world vision of peace and how to achieve it. Integral to this process has been the grassroots movement to create a cabinet level Department of Peace, which has been spearheaded by Rep. Dennis Kucinich (D-OH). Some say this is "pie in the sky" legislation with no hope of ever passing. I say we need visionary out-of-the-box approaches to public policy and a total paradigm shift to tackle the problems of the twenty-first century. Yes, the Department of Peace is an agency whose time has come. The proposed Department of Peace "would have jurisdiction both internationally and domestically." At the international level the bill to create the department would outline specific nonviolent options that the president could use to develop resolutions to conflicts and to create "highly sophisticated peacemaking strategies for post-war stabilization." As much as international stability and conflict resolution are integral to peace, the process of rethinking our policies about war and peace must first begin at home, and that is why the Department of Peace would also have a domestic role to play in developing strategies that address violence—no matter what form it takes. The domestic responsibilities would include addressing local and national issues like hate crimes, violence against women, drug- and gang-related violence, school bullying, and prison reform. The department would coordinate under one umbrella the various government agencies that are currently addressing the issues of violence so that the government could more efficiently and effectively direct change rather than attempting to handle issues of violence in agencies scattered among numerous departments. "The Department of Peace would establish a Peace Academy, patterned after the military academies, where students would learn peaceful conflict resolution skills and, after graduation, would serve in peace-related postings here at home or abroad."

Don't get me wrong now. As I have said, I recognize the threats and dangers of the world. Terrorism is real and must be addressed and eliminated. I am not looking at the world through rose-colored glasses. We must protect our nation and not cause more violence and war as we do. As I said in 2001 on the floor of Congress, "military action will not solve the problems of international terrorism." The world is complex and our foreign and military policies must reflect these complexities by coming up with comprehensive solutions which also get to the root causes of terrorism. And I know that war is not the answer.

Issues of violence, injustice, poverty, political instability, and worldwide pandemics all affect the ability to make and maintain peace. I will continue to make eradicating HIV/AIDS, malaria, ending poverty, and reordering our national budget and spending priorities for education, health care, jobs, and housing rather than building bombs and prisons. And of course I will continue to fight every day for global peace and security. I encourage all Americans to reach out and get involved, contact their local and national representatives, and make their voices heard by our country's leaders. If we fight for justice, then peace can have a chance. Otherwise, we will be destined to be swept up in the mistakes we made in Iraq, Vietnam, and Korea. I will never believe in the blind acceptance of violence as a way of life at home and abroad nor government policies that promote or sanction violence in any form.

There have been many of my contemporaries who have died in the line of duty trying to make this a better world. I have known many of them personally and I think of them everyday. Selfless human beings, such as Rep. Mickey Leland (D-TX) who died in Ethiopia in a plane crash taking food to hungry children. Joyce Williams, my good friend and a beautiful and brilliant young woman who I trained and hired to work for Cong. Ron Dellums (D-CA) perished in that crash along with many other brave souls. I call him the greatest U.S. Secretary of Commerce ever, Ron Brown, who I got to know when he was on Sen. Ted Kennedy's (D-MA) staff in the early 1970s, was killed in a plane crash in Croatia with his dedicated colleagues, many of whom I knew.

All of their deaths and many others whom I have had the privilege to know and work with are no longer with us. Their deaths were like arrows in my heart, so young, so smart, so patriotic.

Little did my mother know that her suffering and the indignities she experienced trying to bring me into the world would become the reason for my existence. Nor did she know that when we left El Paso, Texas, in 1960 I would try to fulfill the words I wrote in my diary: to work each and every day to make this a better world. My life has been tough and difficult with many ups and downs. But it has been a lot of fun. I am convinced that if we come together as a nation, recognize and learn the lessons of the past, then we can create a better future for our children. And, they will never be alone.

Index

abortion, 106, 107, 122–23n1; in China, 39

abstinence-only policies, 38; sexually transmitted diseases, spread of, 37; and teen pregnancies, 37

abstinence-plus policies, 38

affirmative action, 84

Afghanistan, 158, 185

Africa, 81, 85, 150, 153; AIDS in, xv, 112, 116, 117

African Americans, 42; affirmative action, 84; and AIDS, 113; attitudes toward, 82; discrimination toward, 77, 80; and domestic violence, 144; in prison, 189, 190; and Proposition 209, 84; treatment of, 3–4, 86; in United States,

role of in, 87; violence against, 79

Ahasuerus, King. *See* Xerxes the Great

AIDS, 39, 98; in Africa, xv, 112, 116, 117; and African Americans, 113; in developing countries, 114, 115; prevention of, 114, 115; and travel ban, 192; women and girls, 115

Albright, Madeleine, 181

Allen Temple Baptist Church, 33, 34, 117, 185

al-Malaki, Nouri, 70

al-Qaeda, 68, 169

Angelou, Maya, 181

Annenberg School for Communication, 144

Anthony, Susan B., 149

Aristide, Jean Bertrand, 193
Ashe, Arthur, 167
Asia, 150, 153
Asian Pacific American Caucus, 164
Assistance for Orphans and Other Vulnerable Children in Developing Countries Act, 114

Bangkok (Thailand), 192
Barbeque'n With Bobby Seale (Seale), 51
Barcelona (Spain), 192
Barragán, Luis, 200
Barnett, Louis, 154
battered women's syndrome, 126, 137; posttraumatic stress, as form of, 140
Baxter, Nathan, 173, 181
Beatitudes, 27, 63
Bechtel, 153
Belafonte, Harry, 185
Bethune, Mary McLeod, 15
Better, Bill (Barbara Lee's second husband), 133; as abusive, 134–37; death of, 139; mental illness of, 138
Bigthan, 99–100n1
Bill of Rights, 79
bin Laden, Osama, 185
birth control, 105
birth control pill, 105
Black Caucus Faith-Based Task Force, 42

black community: church in, 42; as oppressed colony, 51. *See also* African Americans
black nationalist groups, 58, 59
Black Panther Party, 46, 112, 147; community issues, addressing of, 52, 53; as controversial, 61; as factionalized, 54; and FBI, 59, 60; Free Breakfast for Children Program of, 56, 58; growth of, 54; image of, 53; inclusiveness of, 54; as international organization, 62; Mayfair Supermarket, boycott of, 57; police patrols of, 53; principles of, 47; purpose of, 51, 52; surveillance of, 59; survival programs of, 54, 55, 148; Ten Point Program of, 47, 48, 49, 54, 63, 111; as threat, 58–59
Black Student Union (BSU), 46, 148, 149
Blackwater, 153
Blake, James, 96
Bock, Audie, 179
Bolling v. Sharpe, 80
Bono, xv, 116–17
Boston (Massachusetts), 54
Bouteflika, Abdelaziz, 191
Boyette, Bill, 57, 58
Bradley, Joseph P., 78
Brown v. Board of Education of Topeka, Kansas, 80, 81, 84

Brown, Corrine, 177, 182

Brown, Elaine, 46, 51, 54, 63

Brown, Henry Billings, 79

Brown, Willie, 89

Buchanan, Julia, 28, 82

Bush administration, 75, 93, 163; as above law, 70; and AIDS, 115; faith-based initiatives of, 40; foreign policy of, as militaristic, 66, 73, 74, 158; Hurricane Katrina, response to, 202; as imperialistic, 152; nuclear proliferation, encouraging of, 74; and September 11 attacks, xiv, 65; war-making policies, sanctioning of, 66. *See also* George W. Bush

Bush, George H. W., 173

Bush, George W., xv, 39, 70, 92, 97, 113–14, 153, 160, 173, 177, 192; pre-emptive war doctrine of, 66; and September 11 attacks, 169, 171, 185. *See also* Bush administration

Byron Rumford Fair Housing Act, 83

California, 37, 117, 163; prisons in, 189; Proposition 209 in, 84; segregation in, 83, 84

California Commission on the Status of the African American Male, 189

California Institution for Women, 144

California Rainbow Coalition, 159

CalPERS, 192

Cal State Package Store and Tavern Owners Association (Cal-Pack), 57

Carmichael, Stokely, 58

Carson, Julia, 96–97

Carter, Jimmy, 98, 173

Centers for Disease Control and Prevention (CDC), 112

Central Intelligence Agency (CIA), 152, 171

Chad, 190

Charitable Choice initiative, 41

Cheadle, Don, 191

Cheney, Dick, 153, 160

Chicago (Illinois), 54

child abuse: women, violence against, 24

China, 39, 191

Chisholm, Shirley, xii, xiii, 57, 61, 95, 162; contributions, recognition of, 90, 91; death of, 91; presidential campaign of, 87, 88, 151; as radical, 92; as Renaissance woman, 89; as role model, 87

Church for Today, 31–32

Church for Tomorrow, 46

Civil Rights Act (1875), 78,

Civil Rights Act (1964), 52, 85

Civil Rights Cases, 78
civil rights movement, xi, xii, 92,
   96
Civil War, 78, 170
Clarification of Federal Employees
   Protection Act, 120
Clayton, Eva, 172
Cleaver, Eldridge, 46, 63
Cleaver, Kathleen, 46
Clinton administration:
   "abstinence-only" policy in, 37;
   and Kosovo, xiv, 177
Clinton, Bill, 113, 114, 145, 173
Clinton, Hillary, 142, 163
COINTELPRO, 51, 57, 60, 61;
   Black Panthers, focus of, 59;
   goals of, 58
Common Sense Budget Act, 74
Commonwealth Fund, 144
The Communist Manifesto (Marx),
   47
Community Alert Patrol (CAP),
   52, 53
Community Health Alliance for
   Neighborhood Growth and
   Education (CHANGE, Inc.),
   109, 110; *The Ten Point
   Program*, as modeled after, 111
Community Solutions Act, 40,
   42
Comprehensive Anti-Apartheid
   Act (1986), 153–54
Congress: and presidential powers,
   170

Congressional Black Caucus
   (CBC), 67, 68, 98, 164, 167,
   184, 192
Congressional Black Caucus
   Foundation, 184, 189
Congressional Black Caucus Task
   Force on Global HIV/AIDS, 113
Congressional Progressive Caucus,
   67, 68
Connerly, Ward, 84
Constitution, 79, 118; and
   presidential powers, 170
contraception, 101
Conyers, John, 184
Cooper, Marc, 180
Cosby, Bill, 182, 183
Cosby, Camille, 182
Cuba, 166, 190, 195
Cummins, Elijah, 172

Dalai Lama: on peace, xvi
Danforth, John C., 119
Darfur, 191
Darius, 99–100n1
Daughters of Charity of St.
   Vincent de Paul, 1
Davis, Angela, 46
*Declaration of Principles for a Long-
   Term Relationship of Cooperation
   and Friendship Between the
   Republic of Iraq and the United
   States of America*, 70, 72;
   imperial presidency, as evidence
   of, 71

Dellums, Ron, xii, xiii, 50, 51, 63, 111, 113, 138, 151, 155, 174, 195, 196, 206; charisma of, 153, 196, 206; courage of, 154
Denver (Colorado), 54
Department of Defense (DOD), 69
Department of Peace, 205
Dickerson Employee Benefits, 204
Dickerson, Jean, 178
Domestic Partners Benefits and Obligations Act, 120
domestic violence, 125–26, 146; among black women, 144; child abuse, as form of, 128; public housing, eviction from, 144, 145. See also violence
Douglass, Frederick, 65
Durban (South Africa), 192

Edelman, Marian Wright, 147
Eichler, Joseph, 200
El Paso (Texas), 5, 25, 83, 107
Ensler, Eve, 181
Erikson, Erik, 49
Esther, Queen, 77, 78, 91, 92, 94, 97, 99–100n1
Europe, 84, 85, 150

Fahrenheit 9/11 (film), 159
Faith-Based Task Force, 41
"Fallingwater," 200
Family and Medical Leave Act, 120
Family and Medical Leave Inclusion Act, 120

family violence, 24. See also domestic violence; violence
Fathers Count Act, 40
Federal Bureau of Investigation (FBI), 51, 55, 58, 92, 152; and Black Panthers, 59, 60
Ferguson, John H., 79
First Amendment, 52
Fleischer, Ari, 179–80
Flight 77, 168
Flight 93, 156, 168
Florida, 159
Fonda, Jane, 51
Ford, Gerald, 173
Fountaine, Gwen V., 48, 50
Fourteenth Amendment, 78
"Free Huey" movement, 60

Gaines, Sandy, 88
gay adoption, 120
gay community, 117, 118
Gear Up, 166
genocide, 190, 191, 192, 193
Germany, 71
Ghana, 35, 150
Gibson, Althea, 1
Global Access to HIV/AIDS Medicines Act, 114
Global Access to HIV/AIDS Prevention, Awareness, Education, and Treatment Act, 114

Global Aids Initiative, 114
Global Fund, 113. *See also* World
  Bank AIDS Trust Fund
Global Gag rule, 38, 39. *See also*
  Mexico City Policy
global warming, 193, 194
Global War on Terror, 66, 68
Global Wars of Aggression, 54
Glover, Danny, 183
Glover, Rudy, 111
Gold, Rachel Benson,
  122–23n1
Goodman, Ellen, 181
Gore, Al, 159
Green, Wanda, 172
Greensfelder, Claire, 180
Grenada, 36
Gulf of Tonkin Resolution, 170,
  171, 176
Guttmacher Institute,
  122–23n1

Haiti, 195
Halliburton, 153
Haman, 99–100n1
Harlan, John Marshall, 79–80
Hastert, Dennis, 174
Hayes, Isaac, 35
Helms, Jesse, xv, 98
hip hop community, 160
Hispanic Caucus, 164
Hispanics, xiv. *See also* Latinos
HIV/AIDS Reauthorization Bill,
  192

Holmgren, Janet L., 149
homophobia, 93, 119–20
Hoover, J. Edgar, 58, 59
Horowitz, David, 56, 57, 178
Hotel Rwanda (film), 191
House Appropriations Committee,
  67
House Foreign Relations
  Committee, 98
House International Relations
  Committee, 177
House Judiciary Committee, 151
Houston (Texas), 162
Howell, Jo (Granddad), 127
Howell, Maude Ash, 18, 19, 126,
  127
Hoyer, Steny, 176
Huerta, Dolores, xii, xiv, xv
Huggins, Ericka, 49
Human Rights Caucus, 193
Humphrey, Hubert, 88
Hurricane Katrina, 91, 201; and
  African Americans, 202
Hussein, Saddam, 68
Hyde Amendment, 39
Hyde, Henry, 177

India, 194; and United States,
  74
integration: as vanishing, 84
Internal Revenue Service (IRS),
  152
International AIDS Conference,
  192

International Atomic Energy
Agency, 72
Iran, 66, 68, 158; nuclear weapons
program in, 72, 73
Iran Diplomatic Accountability
Act, 73
Iran Nuclear Authorization Act,
73
Iraq, 177, 189, 206; invasion of,
65, 66, 68, 185; military bases
in, 69, 70; military force
against, authorization of, 66,
68; occupation of, 158; and
weapons of mass destruction,
68
Iraq War, 73, 91, 93, 94, 156, 164;
and fully funded redeployment,
69; funding of, 69
Israel, 35

Jackson, Harry B., 29
Jackson, James, 29
Jackson, Jesse, 162, 182, 183
Japan, 71, 194
Jarrar, Raed, 71
Jesus: as revolutionary, 32
Jesus and the Disinherited
(Thurman), 33
Jews: and Esther, 99–100n1
Jim Crow laws, 79, 82, 97
Johnson, Deborah, 111
Johnson, Eddie Bernice, 182
Johnson, Lyndon B., 170, 175
Jones, Stephanie Tubbs, 177

Jordan, Barbara, 101
Juarez (Mexico), 11, 107

Katzman, Kenneth, 70
Kaufman, Gail, 180
Kennedy, Caroline, 162
Kennedy, Patrick, 162
Kennedy, Ted, 162
Kerry, John, 192
King, Coretta Scott, 92–94
King, Larry, 181
King, Martin Luther, Jr., xiv, 33,
54, 58, 92, 93–94, 96;
assassination of, 132, 133; and
Vietnam War, 67, 75
Korb, Larry, 74
Korea, 206. See also North Korea;
South Korea
Kucinich, Dennis, 205
Ku Klux Klan (KKK), 79
Kyoto Protocol, 194

Lantos, Tom, 171, 176, 177
Lautenberg, Frank R., 38
Leach, Jim, 113
Lebanon, 36
LeClaire, Danielle, 167
Legorreta, Ricardo, 200
Lee Amendment, 145
Lee, Angela, 200
Lee, Barbara, 157; and abortion,
106, 107, 108; and AIDS,
113–17; birth of, 3; Black
Panther Party, involvement in,

46, 50–51, 54–62, 148; and
Black Student Union (BSU),
148, 149; bloodline of, 4;
candidacy of, 155; Catholicism,
conversion to, 28; as
cheerleader, 29, 83, 84, 104;
childhood of, 5, 6, 8, 10, 17–19,
25; and Shirley Chisholm, xiii,
87–91, 151; criticism of, 179;
death threats against, 156, 178;
divorce of, 21, 45, 46; domestic
violence, as victim of, 134–37;
education of, 26–28, 45–46,
80–81, 108–9, 148–51; in
England, 84; family tree of, as
confusing, 19–20; Florida vote,
protest toward, 159; and "food
stamp challenge," 203; in
Ghana, 35, 197–198; and global
warming, 193, 194; in Grenada,
36; in Israel, 35; marriages of,
20, 30, 31, 84, 104–6, 130–33,
136; mentoring, importance of
to, 89; at Mills College,
148–51; miscarriage of, 31, 104;
Nobel Peace Prize nomination
of, 193; Barack Obama,
endorsement of, 162, 165, 166;
and peace movement, 204, 205;
pregnancy of, 29, 30, 104, 105;
as radical, accusations of,
155–56; and religion, 25, 26;
role models of, 77; at San
Fernando High School, 29, 83,
84; as self-conscious, 27; self-
esteem of, 86; self-image of, 11,
12; September 11 attacks,
reaction to, 170–75, 181;
September 11 resolution, vote
against, xiii–xiv, 34, 36, 66,
92–93, 156, 176–77, 184–85,
187; as sexually active, 29;
sexual awakening of, 102, 103;
shame, feelings of, 82; at St.
Joseph's, 26, 27, 28; support of,
182–85; as un-American,
accusations of, 180
Lee, Carl (Barbara Lee's first
husband), 20, 21, 29, 30, 31,
84, 104–6, 128–30; as good-
natured, 131, 132, 137
Lee, Carl (Carl Lee's father), 45
Lee, Carl Anthony (Tony), 10, 45,
128, 200, 204
Lee, Craig, 45, 128, 135, 200, 204
Lee, Memuna, 200, 204
Lee, Peggy (Carl Lee's mother), 45
Lee, Sheila Jackson, 167
Lessons from Before Roe: Will Past
Be Prologue? (Gold), 122
Lewis, James Henderson (Barbara
Lee's biological father), 17, 18,
19; as violent, 126–28, 137
Lewis, John, 177
Lewis, Walter, 126
Local Law Enforcement Hate
Crimes Prevention Act (2005),
121

Los Angeles (California), 52, 54
Los Angeles Police Department, 52
Louisiana: and Act III, 79
Lovett, Robert A., 81
lynchings, 79

Maher, Bill, 179, 180
Malcolm X, 94
Marx, Karl, 47
Maslow, Abraham, 112
Massey, Bill, 8, 17, 29, 80
Mayfair Supermarket: boycott
    against, 57
McCain-Feingold bill, 164
McCain, John, 72, 164
McCraven, Carl, 83
McDaniels, Tom, 168
McGovern, George, 88
McKinney, Cynthia, 174
Meredith, James H., 95
Mexican Revolution, 5
Mexico City Policy, 39. *See also*
    Global Gag rule
Middle East, 35, 68
Mills College, 45, 151; black
    history, as curriculum at,
    149–50; endowed chair at,
    148–49; nurturing atmosphere
    in, 147, 148; student body,
    diversity of, 148; and women's
    causes, 150
Mink, Patsy, 97
Mitchell, Clarence, 81
Mitchell, John, 59

Montgomery Bus Boycott, 96
Moore, Dennis, 168
Moore, Michael, 159
Moore, Stephanie, 168
Mordecai, 99–100n1
Morse, Wayne, 176
Motley, Constance Baker, 95
Mubarak, Mohammed Hosni, 194
Muhammad, Elijah, 58
Mulford, David Donald, 53
Mullins, Fran, 88
Muskie, Edmund, 88

Nadler, Jerrold, 174
Nation of Islam, 58
National Association for the
    Advancement of Colored
    People (NAACP), 83
National Black Church Arts
    Program, 33
National Domestic Violence
    Hotline, 142, 143
National Intelligence Estimate
    (NIE), 72
National Security Agency (NSA),
    193
Native Americans, 78
Negroponte, John, 71
Newark (New Jersey), 54
New Haven (Connecticut), 54
New Orleans (Louisiana), 79
Newton, Huey, 46, 47, 53–54,
    56–58, 88; apartment of, 48;
    death of, 63; description of, 48,

49; discrediting of, 55; exile of, 61; and police, 52; surveillance of, 59

New York (state) 175

New York (New York), 54, 55, 122–23n1

Nicaragua, 153; Contra rebels in, 171

Nightline (television program), 191

Ninth District, xiii, 4, 166

Nixon administration, 151, 152

Nixon, Richard, 48, 152; impeachment of, 151; resignation of, 151

Noonan, Peggy, 181

Northern California Young Democrats, 159

North Korea, 74. *See also* Korea; South Korea

Norwood, Charlie, 174

Nuclear Non-Proliferation Treaty (NPT), 74

Oakland (California), 117, 166; as progressive, 154, 194, 199

Oakland Community Learning Center, 55

Oakland Community School, 56

Oakland Zoo: and Chinese pandas, 190

Obama, Barack, 160, 161, 163, 165; as inspiring, 162

Ohio, 159

Omaha (Nebraska), 54

1000 Women for the Nobel Peace Prize, 193

Oprah Winfrey Show, 181

Out-of-Iraq Caucus, 67, 69

Pacoima Lutheran Memorial Credit Union, 83

Papillion, Juanita, 111

Parish, William W. C. "Papa" (Barbara Lee's maternal grandfather), 15, 19, 25, 26, 102; disappearance of, 20; as extraordinary, 9; as strict, 10; work ethic of, 14

Parish, Willie (Barbara Lee's maternal grandmother), 1, 4, 9, 11, 15, 25; death of, 16; "whiteness" of, 2, 16

Parks, Rosa, xi, xii, xiv, 97; civil rights movement, as mother of, 96

Payne, Don, 184

peace movement, 204, 205

Pelosi, Nancy, 41, 97, 149, 177

Pennsylvania, 156, 168, 175

Pentagon, 168

people of color: as disenfranchised, 159; as majority, 85. *See also* African Americans; Hispanics

Permanent Partners Immigration Act, 120

Personal Responsibility and Work Opportunity Reconciliation Act, 22, 37

Philadelphia (Pennsylvania), 54, 55

The Phillis (ship), 14

Phillis Wheatley Club, 12–13, 14

Plessy v. Ferguson, 79

Plessy, Homère, 79

Poems on Various Subjects (Wheatley), 13

Pointer, Willie. *See* Willie Parish

police discrimination, 52

Politically Incorrect (television program), 179

pollution, 193; and people of color, 194

population growth, 39

poverty, 157, 201, 203; increase in, 202

pre-emptive war doctrine, 65, 72, 73, 94, 190

President's Emergency Plan for AIDS Relief (PEPFAR), 114, 115

Product Red, 116

Progressive Caucus, 164

Protection Against Transmission of HIV for Women and Youth (PATHWAY) Act, 115

Public Safety, Sentencing, and Incarceration Reform Caucus, 189

Purim, 99–100n1

racism: effects of, 87; as institutionalized, 83

Rackley, Alex, 49

Rainbow PUSH Coalition, 182

Rankin, Jeannette, 96

Raskin, Marcus, 174

Rawlings, Jerry, 35

Reading, John, 47

Reagan administration, 171

Reagan, Ronald, 153

Reconstruction, 78

Responsible Education About Life (REAL) Act, 38

Revolutionary Action Movement, 58

Revolutionary Suicide (Newton), 57

Revolutionary War, 14

Rice, Condoleezza, 71

Riles, Wilson, Jr., 88

Roe v. Wade, 101, 122–23n1

Rwanda, 191

same-sex marriage, 118–20

San Diego (California), 54

Sandinistas, 153

San Fernando High School, 29, 83, 84

San Francisco (California), 130, 132

San Jose (California), 132

Saudi Arabia, 74, 75

Sawyer, Diane, 181

Scott, Bobby, 184

Seale, Bobby, xii, 45–49, 51, 58, 63, 88; description of, 50; incarceration of, 61; leadership of, 54

Second Amendment, 52

segregation, 78, 79, 82, 83, 85; as de facto, 84; protest of, 80, 81

Seize the Time: The Story of the Black Panther Party (Seale), 49

September 11 attacks, 36, 66, 167–69, 175; response to, 171, 185, 188

9/11 Commission, 65

sex education, 101, 103

sexual discrimination, 98

sexual orientation: and discrimination, 120–21; and hate crimes, 121; and military, 121; and workplace hiring, 121

Shabazz, Betty, 94–95

Shays, Christopher, 38

Sheldon, Lou, 118

Shirek, Maudelle, 95

Sisters of Loretto, xii, 26, 27, 35, 77

Skelton, Ike, 171

Slaughter, Kieron, 64

slavery, 14, 27–28, 78, 85; as dehumanizing, 86; legacy of, 4, 82, 86, 87

Smith, J. Alfred, Jr., 34, 35

Smith, J. Alfred, Sr., 34, 35

Social Security, 160, 161, 163

Soul on Ice (Cleaver), 46, 63

South: lynching in, 79

South Africa: and AIDS, 192, 193; apartheid in, 93, 153, 154, 192

South America, 150, 153

South Carolina, 162

Southern California, 83

Southern Christian Leadership Conference, 58

South Korea, 71. *See also* Korea; North Korea

Steinem, Gloria, xii, xiv, 181

Stewart, Martha, 142

St. Joseph's school, 26, 27, 28

Student Nonviolent Coordinating Committee, 58

Sudan, 191; Janjaweed in, 191

Sullivan, Andrew, 165

Supreme Court, 78; and abortion, 122–23n1; on segregated schools, 81; and "separate but equal" doctrine, 79, 80

Swanson, Sandré, 88, 172, 178

Taliban, 185

Taylor, Susan, 184

teen pregnancy, 106

Teresh, 99–100n1

terrorism, 65, 205, 206

Thompson, Alice, 64

Thurman, Howard, 33

Toronto (Canada), 192

Traditional Values Coalition, 118

Trio, 166
True Story (magazine), 103, 104
Truth, Sojourner, 25, 95
Tubman, Harriet, 95, 125
Tutt, Beverly (Barbara Lee's sister), 9, 10, 27, 200
Tutt, Evelyn, 6
Tutt, Garvin, 5, 6, 7, 8, 17–19, 129
Tutt, Mildred (Barbara Lee's mother), 1–7, 12, 19–20, 26–27, 29–30, 77, 127, 187, 200, 204, 207; appearance of, 11; education of, 14, 15; marriages of, 8, 18; Phillis Wheatley Club, importance to, 13, 14; work ethic of, 14
Tutt, Mildred (Barbara Lee's sister), 9, 10, 18, 19, 26, 27, 50, 128, 200
Tutt, Reiko, 7, 8, 129
Tutu, Desmond, 34, 180

Underground Railroad, 95
United Farm Workers Union, xiv
United Nations, 115; and AIDS, 116; weapons of mass destruction, inspection for, 68
United Nations Population Fund, 39
United States, 39, 75, 153, 193, 194; attitude toward, 158; crime in, 189; and India, 74; lynching in, 79; poverty in, 157; prison

system of, 188, 189; respect, lack of toward, 158; status-of-forces agreements of, 71, 72
Upper Heyford (England), 84
Upward Bound, 166

Van Tanner, Betty, 57
Vietnam, 67, 206
Vietnam War, 67, 75, 153, 170, 176
violence, 203, 205, 206; against black women, 144; and control, 142; as cyclical, 140; against female teenagers, 142–43; as generational, 141; negative financial repercussions of, 143; as repetitive, 140, 141; against women, 24, 125–26, 139, 140, 141, 142, 143. *See also* domestic violence; family violence
Violence Against Women Act, 22, 144
Virginia, 175
Voltaire, 13

Walker, Alice, 183, 187
Walters, Barbara, 181
War Powers Resolution (1973), 170
Warwick, Dionne, 35
Washington, George, 13
Watergate, 151, 152, 153
Waters, Maxine, 69, 182, 184
Watson, Diane, 167

Wattleton, Faye, 181
Watt, Mel, 184
Watts riot, 52
Wayne Morse Integrity in Politics Award, 176
W. C. Parish Co., 154
Weiner, Andrew, 75
welfare reform, 22, 23, 37, 38
welfare system, 22; as safety net, 129
Wert, President, 150
West Africa, 35
Wexler, Robert, 75
Wheatley, John, 13
Wheatley, Phillis, 13, 95
Wheatley, Susanna, 13
Williams, W. Hazaiah, 32, 33, 35
Williamson, Marianne, 181
Wilson, Pete, 21, 84, 118, 144, 154

Winfrey, Oprah, 77, 181, 182
women, 163; and affordable housing, 144, 145; as devalued, 126, 142; homelessness among, 144; violence against, 24, 125–26, 140–45; violence against, psychological effects of, 139
women's movement, xiv
Woolsey, Lynn, 69, 74, 98, 174
World AIDS Conference, 116
World Bank AIDS Trust Fund, 113. *See also* Global Fund
World Health Organization (WHO), 115
World Trade Center, 168
Wright, Frank Lloyd, 200

Xerxes the Great, 99–100n1

Younger Voter Project, 160

❧

About the Author

Barbara Lee was first elected to represent California's Ninth Congressional District in 1998. In 2005, she was nominated for the Nobel Peace Prize along with women from 150 countries as part of the international project 1000 Women for Peace. She lives in Oakland, California, and Washington, DC.